Praise for
You Are a Heroine:
A Retelling of the Hero's Journey

You Are a Heroine is an operating manual containing all a woman needs to navigate her personal journey. Susanna Liller brings myth and theory to life with examples from the lives of real people, including the author, and well thought-out tasks and exercises the reader can use to claim her identity and her place in the world. Use it as a GPS. Refer to it often.

Patricia R. Adson, Ph.D. LP, coach and psychotherapist

You would think that a book entitled *You Are a Heroine* would be a beacon for women who want to step out of the comfort zone society fashioned for them—and of course it is. This book is a roadmap for any woman who is ready to claim the day. But this is *also a very useful book for men* who want to better understand the complex journey women have endured for so long—a journey that menfolk can be all but oblivious to. This is a very special era, a time when a deeper truth is finally coming forth. Susanna Liller's brave book presents this truth in a way we can all understand.

Jack Barnard, writer and creativity coach

You Are a Heroine provides women with important knowledge about the transformative path they walk, while Susanna Liller teaches us about the heroine's journey in a readable, accessible and real-life way. My focus is helping women become bigger players in the marketplace. This book will help all women become bigger players in life.

Bonnie Marcus, author of *The Politics of Promotion*

Susanna Liller came into my life when I was at a critical juncture, stuck professionally, without a clue as to how to move forward. Through her coaching, I found the strength to take the leap from a miserable, but well-paid, job to starting my own business. Now she is sharing her expertise, wisdom and good humor in this brilliant book. It will benefit any woman who wants to step out of her cookie-cutter role, yet faces daunting challenges. Following Susanna's guidance, readers will come to know that there is a larger framework in which they're operating, a framework that's shaping them into strong, wise change agents in today's world.

Catherine Fellenz, retired change manager

With so many distractions and choices to sort through, it's not easy to land on the right life path *for you*. Susanna Liller, a gifted coach and mentor to women, is your sure-footed guide through the overwhelm and into a place of confidence, calm and clarity. No matter what your circumstances or obstacles, reading this book will ease the challenge of finding a way in the world that feels fully resonant and richly rewarding.

Amy Wood, Psy.D., author of *Life Your Way*

In *You Are a Heroine*, Susanna Liller takes you by the hand to the edge of your heroine's journey and sends you off with a map of the signposts you'll encounter, to know you're never lost. This book serves as a worthy guide to living to the fullest the great story that is your life.

Gail Larsen, author and teacher,
Transformational Speaking

You Are a Heroine connects every woman to her strong, courageous and transformative self at a time when we all need to be reminded of our resilient nature. In a consistently convincing way, author Susanna Liller sends us the message that our best selves are only a journey away. Her book deliberately describes the Heroine's path in universal and manageable steps and provides a "you can do it" theme as a backdrop. With her personal anecdotes and real life examples of Heroines' journeys, Susanna conveys the truth: that any woman can embark on this challenging journey and emerge whole and transformed as she arrives back home to herself.

Barbara Babkirk, master career counselor

In her book, *You Are a Heroine*, Susanna Liller gently nudges us out of our comfort zone and into a place of deeper listening. She helps us to identify our profoundest truths and then inspires the courage and action necessary to honor them. Her expert guidance compels us all to leap—to embrace a life of greater authenticity, satisfaction, and joy.

Jennifer Richard Jacobson, author of *The Dollar Kids*

Is life getting uncomfortable? A persistent voice is calling you to let go of the known and take a different route. You are attracted by this calling, yet something is not allowing you to move... This is the book for you. The warm voice of Susanna Liller will fill you with confidence and shine a light on the blessings that lie ahead. Trust your intuition. If you are reading this, you are a heroine and all you need to know to embark in your heroic journey is here.

Blanca Vergara, author of *One Couple Two Careers*

You Are a Heroine

YOU ARE A HEROINE
A Retelling of the Hero's Journey

by Susanna Liller

EMERALD LAKE
BOOKS

For my Hungarian grandmother, Susanna Banyay
Minden szerelmemmel és hálával

Contents

Preface

It was a blustery November day in 1911 as a passenger train pulled out of the frenzied station in Budapest, Hungary. It was quickly gaining speed when a suitcase suddenly came hurtling out of the train's door. Moments later, a wide-eyed young lady in long skirts leaped from that moving train. A moving train! After picking up her suitcase and wiping it off with the edge of her skirt, the young lady walked shakily back to the station.

Despite what you may think, this is not the story of a fictitious Heroine. No, she was a real woman—a woman who happened to be my grandmother and namesake. She wasn't a daredevil or a stuntwoman. Rather, she was a twenty-one-year-old bound for America to join her fiancé. But she was leaving behind everything familiar: her family, her friends and her country. It was a bitter-sweet parting from her native Hungary.

I'm sure she was nervous, frightened, lonely and excited.

She had only just begun her journey, traveling (alone!) from her quiet village to the bustling city of Budapest to take a train to Amsterdam.

So when the train pulled out of the station and she realized that she had boarded the *wrong* train, she did what anyone following her dream would do—she ran to the still-open door, threw her suitcase out before her, and jumped… right out of that moving train!

I think of my grandmother as a real-life Heroine, but while she is special to me, she's not unique in her Heroine status. You don't have to leap from a moving train to be a Heroine. There are Heroines everywhere you look, as well as in the mirror. And before you dismiss me for saying that you (yes, you!) are a Heroine, let me show you what I mean. You might be surprised.

Introduction

This book is about something that is old—really old... thousands of years old. Yet this *something* is stunningly valuable for our modern lives.

This ancient something is a particular type of story pattern that is found everywhere, in all civilizations and throughout the centuries. As old as it is, it is still as relevant to us today as it was way back when stories were told orally, before they were written down. This type of story delivers a vital life message—a message so important that it has withstood the test of time. To understand this enduring story pattern and its personal connection to us is crucial to the development of ourselves and our society. That's why it was placed in stories in the first place. What better way to transmit a message that needs to be shared and remembered than in a story?

And guess what? The tradition worked! The story pattern is still with us today, in books and films. The story that I'm talking about is the story of the hero or, more specifically, the Hero's Journey story pattern. The Hero's Journey is about what makes the hero a hero: how an ordinary person evolves into someone extraordinary.

Although the story pattern has been around for millennia, it was Joseph Campbell, author and mythologist, who popularized the idea of the Hero's Journey in 1949 with his book *The Hero with a Thousand Faces*. In it, Campbell traces the story of the hero's journey and transformation through the mythologies of the world and demonstrates that, in these stories, the heroes all encounter similar steps, or milestones, on their journeys. But the most important concept to the book that you're holding in your hands right now is that Campbell believed that those same milestones of the Hero's Journey could be applied to us... to our everyday lives.

These milestones are why I wrote this book. The story of the hero is about you; it's about me. It's *our* story. We are heroes and heroines! It doesn't matter how fantastical the stories are. Their core remains the same—the pattern of the hero progressing through the journey is the pattern of how you progress in your life.

Now here is an important clarification: my book is for women. Yes, I could continue to call you a hero, ignoring the term "heroine." But I believe women don't hear enough about themselves in the feminine. This book is about the *Heroine's* Journey. It is designed to awaken the Heroine in you.

The plot of the Heroine's Journey is this: a seemingly ordinary person has an experience that moves her from her known world to a very different world. There she meets all kinds of challenges that culminate in some sort of monumental task, like dragon slaying, killing an evil wizard, destroying a ring of power, or vanquishing a witch to get her broomstick! This task transforms the ordinary person into a more fully realized human being who has a new awareness of herself and her capabilities. The Journey births her into who she really has been all along—a Heroine.

You can experience the milestones of the Heroine's Journey in your own life if (and this is a big *if*) you're willing to leave the safety of your comfort zone. It's not much of a story or a real-life transformation if a Heroine just stays in the same, safe environment. What if Dorothy had stayed on Aunt Em's farm in Kansas? She might have escaped the scary parts in the story, like those flying monkeys, but she also wouldn't have experienced Oz and its wonderful discoveries. Only when we take risks can we begin to break through our personal limitations and truly grow.

Even though this Heroine's Journey story pattern is ancient, it is still relevant to your life today—to the life of a modern twenty-first-century woman—and it still brings many benefits. Do you see it? By viewing your life from the Heroine's perspective, you gain the following:

- *You obtain a model for your development.* You learn to identify the milestones along the way so that you can track your progress on the Journey, making the unknown a little less frightening.

- *You learn to recognize the positive in what appears to be negative.* The hardships of the Journey shape—even birth—you into a wiser woman.

- *You discover that everyone is on a Journey.* You're not traveling alone. Many have traveled the same route before you.

- *You realize your commonalities with others.* The mythical and real-life stories reveal that we all search for truth, whether it is truth about ourselves or truth about the world in which we live.

- *You build confidence and self-esteem when you acknowledge your own Heroine story.* You see things in yourself that you might not have noticed before. You value yourself and your Journey more. You're empowered because you learn you've been a Heroine all along.

- *You learn that life is about the Journey.* The most important thing is your willingness to take that Journey, to move out of your comfort zone and embrace the life-altering changes that ensue.

The point of the Heroine's Journey is to birth you into your real self, the self you may have been holding back. The Journey helps you get past your fears. It helps you recognize the unique gifts you have to offer.

None of this is simple. It is challenging to risk being your unique self. It's also culturally atypical. This is why it's important that we learn to trust and respect our feminine nature and how we do the Journey, distinct from the masculine model. When we can give ourselves permission to fully be ourselves, both in our lives and in our leadership practices, we make a real positive impact on the world.

The Heroine's Journey is about our transformation as women. My mission as a coach, teacher and author is to help you recognize the utility, power and wisdom of this simple yet powerful life message, elegantly ensconced within a story framework so that you can chart your life, get your bearings and flourish.

How to Read This Book

In the first two chapters, you'll learn the context of the Heroine's Journey and receive some useful things to take on the Journey, including a map. You'll also be introduced to three Heroines who'll be traveling with you. In chapters 3 to 7, you'll find yourself traversing the first Journey steps, chapter by chapter. In chapter 8 ("You Own the Perfect Compass"), you'll be given a Task that can help you determine where to focus your life and how to find your direction. This exercise will be very helpful as you travel the Heroine's Journey, but for some, the Task may feel like a distraction from learning the Journey milestones. If you want, you can skip this chapter and continue on, but I highly recommend that you return to complete the Task at some point! In the last chapters, you'll learn about the remaining Journey steps, as well as what life looks like after the Journey. The subsequent components of the book include information to support you on your Journey.

So, are you ready to get reading and to start uncovering who you really are? You're going on the identity search of a lifetime. I think you'll love what you discover!

Chapter 1

It's Not Just a Story, It's Your Life

Awaken your spirit to adventure;
Hold nothing back, learn to find ease in risk;
Soon you will be home in a new rhythm,
For your soul senses the world that awaits you.

—John O'Donohue, *For a New Beginning*

The Heroine's Journey, like any Journey narrative, is made up of a series of stages, also called "milestones." It begins with the main character in her ordinary situation, in regular old life. **Ordinary Life** is what Joseph Campbell called it. The Heroine is going about her usual business. Then something occurs to take her out of that ordinary situation. It may be something external, like a natural disaster. Or it may be an inner urge to go somewhere and do something different. There are many internal and external incidents that push us out of our old patterns, ruts and routines. In Heroine's Journey parlance, this is labeled the **Call**.

The Heroine can heed the Call or refuse it. Usually, if she **Refuses the Call** (which happens a lot), the Call gets louder and more insistent. Think of a wake-up call, which can be most unpleasant. During this unsettled time, the Heroine begins to hear many voices, both her own and others'. People often come forward, voicing their critiques of the Heroine. *You can't do this! You don't know how! You're not smart enough, strong enough or brave enough!* These warnings and admonitions can also come forward in the Heroine's own thoughts. *I can't do this. I will fail. She will do it better than I can.* And so on.

These are the voices of the **Threshold Guardians**, those who want to keep the Heroine back in the same old place they're used to seeing her, her comfort zone. If she answers the Call—grows, leaves, leaps—they'll feel threatened, inadequate, insecure and lonely. Or maybe they're just concerned for her and want her to stay safe, in the way that *they* define safe. Regardless of whether it's out of concern or insecurity, the Threshold Guardians are skilled at planting doubt in the Heroine's mind. (And the most harmful doubt for a Heroine is when she doubts her own inner knowing.)

Thankfully, there are also people who support and encourage the Heroine. *You can do this! Yes, we've been waiting for you to take this step! You set a great example for the rest of us!* These people are called **Mentors** or **Magical Helpers**, and like Threshold Guardians, they can appear at any time during the Journey.

Eventually, when the Heroine can no longer Refuse the Call by ignoring it, she must respond, though responding looks different for everyone. It can be a small step for some and a big jump for others. It can be hovering on or near the Threshold for a long time or taking five steps forward and ten steps back. This step into the unknown, however the Heroine takes it, is called **Crossing the Threshold**. The Heroine is moving into new territory, leaving the comfort zone of her old life, and traversing an imaginary Threshold into an adventure.

The Threshold Crossing is what I call a **Leap**. It's that moment of, *OK, I may be scared, uncertain and doubtful of my abilities, but I'm going to do this because I know it's what I need to do for me!*

I call it a Leap because it's a sudden, often forceful movement into a new "place." It takes energy and courage for the Heroine to leave what she's used to and to try something new, whether it's actually *new terrain* (like a new job or a new place to live) or a *new way of being in the world* (such as choosing a different attitude about something, letting go of an uncomfortable relationship, or opening up to a new one).

It's a Leap because the Heroine is crossing over into the unknown, into the void, over the chasm of uncertainty. And because it's unknown, she's often enveloped in fear. It can be scary, but it can also feel exciting. In terms of personal growth, stretching and embracing change is a necessary step in the Heroine's development. It's almost always about acknowledging herself and her own inner voice—who *she* is and what *she* wants, not what *others* want for her.

The Heroine's Journey is ultimately all about the Heroine allowing herself to become herself.

Unfortunately, after the Leap, things don't necessarily get easier.

Once the Heroine has cleared the Threshold, she's on the road of her new Journey. This time period can have all kinds of trials, false starts, failures and successes. It can be like a maze. *Oops, a dead end! Wrong way! Go back to that fork in the road and turn left, not right.* In Journey terms, this period, when the Heroine experiences lots of turmoil, is called the **Belly of the Whale**. It's all about the Heroine being shaken up and tossed around as if she had been swallowed into a whale's belly. (Campbell's use of this term originates from the biblical story of Jonah, who was swallowed by a whale as part of his Hero's Journey.)

Getting tossed around ultimately aids the Heroine in becoming more herself. Many a Heroine has erroneous beliefs about herself that limit her expectations for her life. However, working through challenges and finding ways to recover from mistakes is how she learns. It's about her unfolding into her fullest self and not staying small. Like the proverbial oyster, she needs the grit of the sand to make the pearl.

The Heroine also meets **Dragons** while on the Journey. Dragons are deep-seated and challenging beliefs or baggage that the Heroine has been carrying around for most of her life— baggage and beliefs that eventually become roadblocks on the Heroine's Journey. The Journey illuminates them and offers the Heroine the opportunity to understand, heal and then dispense with them. (Often, heroes are pictured as fighting dragons. However, what I've found from working with women is the more feminine tendency to *befriend* their Dragons! If they take the time to understand how that roadblock originated, women are more prone to understand, transform and integrate an old fear, rather than slay it.)

Fear-based Dragons are much more insidious than the Threshold Guardians. They go deeper—often back to childhood, where erroneous beliefs can take root. Without her awareness, they run the Heroine's life. Her internal voices shout at her, *I can't trust myself. I can't do it by myself. This isn't safe! I will be abandoned if I do that! I will become unlovable…*

The Heroine must persevere to make it through the Belly of the Whale and to conquer (or befriend) her Dragons. Once the Heroine has done this, her next responsibility is to **Cross the Return Threshold** back to her home or place of business or wherever she has her community. She then shares the rewards she gained from this particular Journey. The rewards are known as **Gifts Received** and could be new levels of skill or awareness, more confidence, spiritual growth, financial achievement and so on. The Gifts that a Heroine receives from her hard and heroic work on her Journey can help everyone. Consider the woman who has taken the Journey to free herself from a dependent or abusive relationship or the woman who took the Journey to accept a difficult role in a new job. The strengths and skills gained by such women will benefit those around her. The Journey is a personal experience, but this expansion of herself also improves society.

The last milestone on the Heroine's Journey is the **Freedom to Live**. The Heroine has released, healed or integrated some aspect of herself (a belief, relationship, assumption or misperception) that has kept her from becoming her true self. She now has the freedom to be who she really is. This is the ultimate goal of the Heroine's Journey: to urge, challenge and push each woman into realizing her authentic self and to grow that self into its full potential. Yes, she will be vulnerable during the Journey—she will have to confront difficult situations. But ultimately, if she believes in herself and trusts the process, the Gift of learning to be herself is worth every step she takes on the Journey.

Although it may feel like it, life isn't a bunch of random moments. Those seemingly random moments actually form the time-honored Heroine's Journey. But sometimes you can't see the pattern until you stand back… way back… from a current Journey or until you look back at Journeys you've taken in the past. Every change and challenge that seems random is just a new Journey opportunity.

Our Heroine's Journey is a pattern underlying human experience. It is about transformation and growth. We go through many Journeys in a lifetime. Every Leap in response to a Call signals a new Journey. And we can be on simultaneous Journeys in different areas of our lives. Every change, challenge or situation that confronts us with something new is a potential Journey if we decide to answer the Call. Our Journeys can be confusing and painful, but they bring opportunities for discovery and growth. We develop confidence, understanding and perspective on the Journey. It's a process of self-discovery and self-integration.

What about You?

Who are you? Where are you going?

No matter how you answer those questions, you have the Heroine's Journey as your centering tool. You can use it as a way to put your life in context, to observe it from a higher level. Your Journey opens you up to seeing your life in a new light. It has the power to transform negatives into positives.

Instead of feeling shame or guilt and thinking something like, *I've really messed up the last three years,* the Heroine's Journey can help you see a different perspective. *I was flailing around in the Belly of the Whale, and I certainly learned a lot.*

Instead of beating yourself up for procrastination, the Heroine's Journey can help you instead see that you are receiving, and perhaps refusing, a call. Maybe you're simply not yet ready to cross that threshold.

Instead of making you fear the future and worry about where you are headed, the Heroine's Journey reassures you that you're on a time-honored, well-documented path. If you do your part, it will not let you down.

Chapter 2

Don't Forget Your Silver Shoes (And Other Useful Things for Your Journey)

At that moment Dorothy saw lying on the table the silver shoes that had belonged to the Witch of the East.

"I wonder if they will fit me," she said to Toto. "They would be just the thing to take a long walk in, for they could not wear out."

She took off her old leather shoes and tried on the silver ones, which fitted her as well as if they had been made for her.

Finally, she picked up her basket.

"Come along, Toto," she said. "We will go to the Emerald City and ask the Great Oz how to get back to Kansas again."

She closed the door, locked it and put the key carefully in the pocket of her dress. And so, with Toto trotting along soberly behind her, she started on her journey.

— L. Frank Baum, *The Wizard of Oz*

You're a Heroine. You are on the Heroine's Journey. But if you're new to the idea, then it probably means you have some things to learn. So come with me. I have lots to share with you in this chapter, including a Journey map, the Journey Guidelines and two Tasks to help you begin to see yourself as the Heroine you really are. I'll also introduce you to some other real-life Heroines.

But first, let's be sure we're clear on the meaning of *Heroine*. I'm not talking about Wonder Woman here!

Originally, the word *hero* didn't mean someone of superhuman strength. The typical heroic myth presents the hero as the founder of something: a new age, a new religion, a new city, a new way of life… The hero has to let go of the old in order to find something new—an action that requires a quest.

To be a Heroine, you don't have to leap tall buildings in a single bound or save people on the battlefield. Rather, you only have to let go of something—some old way of being, of living—in order to create something new within you or your life. That's what makes you a Heroine. You develop confidence, understanding and perspective from each Journey you take.

Over the years, and with the help of the many women I've worked with, I've developed my own personal definition of a Heroine.

> A Heroine is a woman who dares to be herself, has stuck out her neck and has taken risks… big or small. She is a woman who is willing to leap and stretch herself, coming out of her comfort zone on a regular basis to try new things, to challenge herself, to do what she has to do even if it scares her—even if it scares her a lot.

No, you're not Wonder Woman. You're a Heroine.

Please wake up to your own "bigness"! The world needs all the Heroines it can get!

Now, I want to give you a few things to assist you on your Journey. First, the map you see on the next page. It traces the route that the Heroine's Journey takes us on.

You can download your own copy to fill in with your life's milestones at susannaliller.com/youareaheroine.

The second thing I want to give you is a set of guiding principles for your Journey.

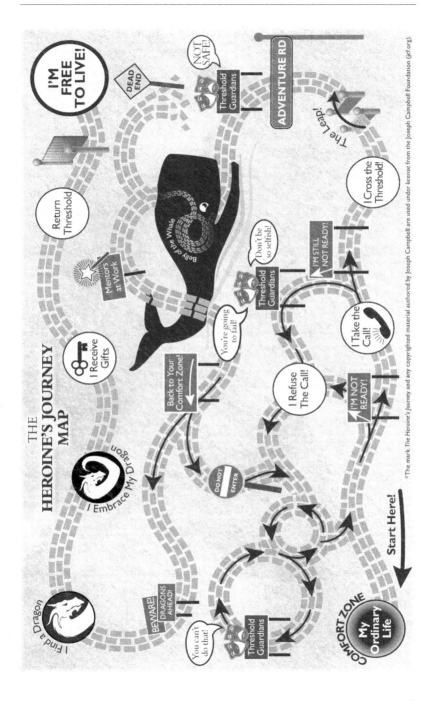

Guidelines for the Road

- Accept yourself… whoever and wherever you are right now.
- Remember, you always have the power to choose. Sure, I'll be asking you to leave your comfort zone, but you can always go back whenever you want.
- Emotion is OK! Feelings can come up, and I hope you can just let them be. Don't try to chase them away. They might point you in the right direction. Practice thinking to yourself, *Hmmm, why did this feeling come up, and what is it telling me?*
- Watch out for critics (internal or external)—those Threshold Guardians who want to judge you and others. The *only* voice that matters for this Journey is yours.
- Comparing yourself to others is pointless. You're doing the Journey your own way.
- Know that you are just where you need to be.
- It's OK not to know where you're going next. Sometimes you sit in limbo for a while. Sometimes it's just about taking a rest.
- It's a process. It can be untidy. There may be dead ends and wrong turns.
- Trust the process. Trust the Journey. Just why has this story pattern been included in so many tales, in all cultures, throughout time? Why is it central to literary heritage all over the world? It's because it has something to teach us.

OK, you are equipped with your map and your guidelines. Just step right over that Threshold.

What? You don't feel comfortable?

I know. That's normal. I've told you that being a Heroine involves stretching and taking risks—Crossing a Threshold from a known world to an unknown world. It doesn't necessarily feel comfortable. Sometimes, we choose a course of action that brings us to our threshold, but other times we're brought there unwillingly. It's up to us what we make of it.

The Heroine's Journey helps us see our struggles and triumphs from a new perspective. Whatever your situation, you can say, *I know this is tough, even frightening, but it's part of my growth. It's my Journey on a road that many have traveled before me. I will receive Gifts from this Journey, and I will be able to share them with others, helping them on their own Journeys.*

And remember, you're not alone on the road. You're in the company of other remarkable, unique, trailblazing Heroines!

If you're sitting there looking at this page, if you've come this far, then there is a part of you that believes you're a Heroine, even though your conscious self might not recognize it. I know that voice inside your head is likely saying, *I'm not a Heroine.* She *may be, but I'm not.*

All of us have that voice in our heads. Hello, Threshold Guardians—that conglomeration of all those familiar voices that have warned us, belittled us, feared for our safety, kept our expectations low so we wouldn't be disappointed, envied us, threatened us, even loved us. Some of you may refer to these voices as your "inner critic." It's these voices that try to keep us small and seemingly nonheroic.

For now, tell those voices, *Thanks for sharing, but please take a back seat.* Then, back to you. Where do you think you are on this Journey?

It may seem unclear. *I think I'm facing a Dragon in my work life, yet I'm hearing a Call in my relationship life.*

That's the way it works. I'll be taking you through the milestones sequentially, but know that you may be in different Journey places in different areas of your life. But there will be one area you'll find yourself focusing on as you read this book. It'll be the part of your life that wants attention *right now.*

It may involve one of your life's roles:

- Parent
- Career person
- Lover
- Daughter
- Friend
- Entrepreneur
- Creator/artist
- Social activist

Some area of your life is calling to you, and the way to begin is to… just listen. Go quiet. What part of your life is speaking to you?

Do you hear it? Keep listening.

While you're sitting there quietly, I'd like you to meet three other Heroines, to help you remember that you don't have to do this alone. Let me tell you a bit about them, and then they'll be sharing some of their Journey stories as we go through the Journey steps together.

Meet Pamela, Maureen and Lisa. (You can read more about them at the back of the book or download the audio of our complete interviews as well as other related resources at susannaliller.com/youareaheroine.)

Pamela McCreary

I met Pamela at my son's wedding. We got into one of those conversations that made us feel like we'd known each other forever, even though we had just met. Among other things, she's an award-winning author. You'll hear her story soon enough, but for now, know that if she were sitting next to you, it would feel as though you'd found a new friend.

Maureen Manley

Maureen is a former member of the U.S. Women's Cycling Team and a skilled speaker and life coach. She and I attended a retreat together. When I met her, I was blown away by the story of her Heroine's Journey. After a Call pushed her across the Threshold, she had to make the huge Leap of reinventing herself.

Lisa Chu

Lisa and I met when we both signed up to be certified to teach a course. She was a former medical doctor and venture capitalist who had started a music school. I fell in love with her story and was captivated by her open and sharing nature.

These brief introductions only give you a glimpse into who these women are. You'll learn more about them as they tell their stories throughout the book; two of them became sidetracked following the wishes of others, the third started on her Heroine's Journey because of a Call that broadsided her.

But for now...

Imagine the five of us sitting together in a circle: Lisa, Maureen, Pamela, you and me. We're in an inviting, relaxed place. You can imagine your own space or you can use mine, a place with wide pine floors, freshly painted cream-colored walls, and a high ceiling. There's a vase of flowers on the low table in the center of the room. A candle is lit. The windows are open and a warm sea breeze is making the curtains dance. Outside, a wind chime sings. We hear the cry of seagulls. We're relaxed, open and ready to go on this Journey together.

Oh, yes. You're going! Why else did you buy this book?

So, let's get started...

The first step on your Journey involves completing two Tasks. *Tasks?* you ask.

Yes. You know, the Heroine is always given tasks to complete on her quest. Dorothy in *The Wizard of Oz* had to get the broomstick of the Wicked Witch of the West. Hercules had twelve tasks, or labors, that were all pretty much impossible! And yes, of course, he completed them.

Fear not! I won't send you to the witch or to do impossible labors, but I want you to start with two Tasks. (Another author might call these *exercises*, but we're Heroines. We do Tasks.)

Task One: The Past Leaps Challenge

The Past Leaps Challenge is a confidence booster. You're going to review previous Threshold Crossings that you have taken in order to help yourself remember that you have made Leaps across the Threshold before—before you even knew it was a big milestone step in the Heroine's Journey.

It's simple. First, list at least three times in your past that you have Crossed the Threshold to begin a Journey (i.e., moved *way out* of your comfort zone).

I moved way out by...	How I felt before and during...	How I felt after (what I gained)...

Second, affirm what it took for you to make those crossings.

When I made those Threshold Crossings, I exhibited these skills and/or qualities:

1. _____

   _____

2. _____

   _____

3. _____

   _____

Task Two: Milestones of My Heroine Journey's Story

This is an ongoing Task. You'll begin it now and add to it as you read this book. This Task will help you familiarize yourself with the Journey and its terminology. Use the prompts in the template on the next page to write or jot down the highlights of your Heroine's Journey on a separate sheet of paper. Notes or outlines are fine.

The goal of this Task is to have you start *writing* your story. You don't have to be a great writer. You are just getting it down on paper. Go ahead! Fit your own story into the milestones. It can be one that's happening now or one you went through in the past. See what happens. Read it to someone. What's that person's reaction? How do you feel about it?

Parameters for Writing

- You can write a past or present-day story.
  - If it's in the past, write about a time when you went through the Heroine Journey's milestones.

○ If it's a present-day story, write about where you currently are on the Heroine's Journey—we just won't know the ending... or, as you're writing your story, you could imagine your best ending.

- You are the main character in the story. You are the Heroine.
- You can invent characters if you want.
- You can embellish.
- You can tell it as a fairy tale or fable. *"Once upon a time, there was a woman named..."*

Go ahead, start writing! Here's a template to guide you:

Milestones of the Journey Template

Milestone	Your Heroine's Journey
Ordinary Life	Where are you right now in your life? What does your comfort zone look like or feel like? How do you spend your days?
The Call	Are you feeling a nudge or a more direct call? Is your current situation making you restless, uncomfortable and dissatisfied? Are others pushing you to do something?
Refusal of the Call	Are you resisting change or a pull to do something different? Is fear holding you in your comfort zone? Do you find yourself coming up with reasons to stay just where you are?

Milestone	Your Heroine's Journey
Threshold Guardians	Are the Threshold Guardians offering their "helpful" advice and warnings? "Who do you think you are?" "You can't do that!" "What will happen to me if you leave?" "You only think about yourself!" "You won't make any money."
Meeting Your Mentors	Who around you is interested in you as a person or in your path of growth and development? Is someone urging you to stretch yourself?
Crossing the Threshold (The Leap)	Are you on the verge of stepping out and trying something different, new, scary, bold? Is life about to change for you?
The Belly of the Whale (The Road of Adventure)	Perhaps you've leapt and you're encountering all kinds of adventures on your new path. It feels a little messy. Good things are happening to you as well as things you didn't expect, and you're having to deal with them. What's going on?
Meeting Your Dragon	Has some old baggage come up from your inner depths that you know you have to deal with to become your best self?

Milestone	Your Heroine's Journey
The Return Threshold	How have you been transformed? How do you share your new understanding and self with the world?
Gifts Received	What are the gifts you've received as a result of taking that Leap?
Freedom to Live	How does it feel to be able to live as your true self?

If you're an especially visual person, you may want to go back to the Heroine's Journey map and note the significant events and decisions that have served as milestones along your way. This will serve to remind of you how far you have already come! You can download a copy of the map template at susannaliller.com/youareaheroine.

Just to remind you, Heroine's Journey Tasks are never pointless. They're not just busy work. Completing these two Tasks shifts you into seeing yourself and your life differently.

- They help you look back and learn to recognize the positives in what could appear to be negative. You have left your comfort zone before. You have *already* leaped! Thus, need I say it again? You are a Heroine.

- They let you see your own Journey on paper, which helps you learn the milestones so that you're more apt to recognize them the next time around.

- They let you see yourself with a more current lens. Sometimes we still keep seeing ourselves through our old lens. *(I'm a loser, and that's all I'll ever be.)* When we've grown beyond that role, we can't always see our own growth.

- They allow you to practice seeing your full potential.

- They acknowledge *you*. As one of our real-life Heroines,

Lisa Chu, told me, "I haven't had sufficient space and time to acknowledge myself along the way... I was both surprised and filled with pride to hear the clarity and power in my own voice. Sometimes we forget to step back and listen to ourselves. We forget to enjoy who we are."

- They help you to see how courageous you really are!

- They help you acknowledge your Heroineism. And when you do that, others can hear you and recognize their own Journey's stories—and learn from you.

So now you have your map, your guidelines and some friends for the road. You've taken a little quiet time to sit and ponder your Journey. Let's not forget that you're well underway with your first two Journey Tasks—and you're acquiring more confidence as you keep putting one foot in front of the other on your Journey. Now... on to Ordinary Life.

Chapter 3

We *Are* Still in Kansas, Toto

Ordinary Life

The usual hero adventure begins with someone from whom something has been taken, or who feels there's something lacking in the normal experiences available or permitted to the members of his society. This person then takes off on a series of adventures beyond the ordinary, either to recover what has been lost or to discover some life-giving elixir. It's usually a cycle, a going and a returning.

Joseph Campbell, *The Power Of Myth*

The Heroine's Journey is a journey of self-discovery, and it's a journey of self-fulfillment... You just have to be a person who feels in some way "less than." And for each of us, the journey is about finding those pieces of us that are "less than" and then giving them the power to be "greater than."

Pamela McCreary, *Real-Life Heroine*

Ordinary Life is how things are before you Cross the Threshold and go on your Journey. It's whatever you consider to be "normal life."

Usually, this looks like some form of:

- making it work.
- trying to fit in.
- idling.

It could also be as bad as... tuning out life.
Then again, it could look like:

- things are going great.
- you are going with the flow.

Calls come and urge you, sometimes vehemently, to do or *be* something different. There is something that needs to happen or that you need to learn in order to grow. Often, when the Call comes, you don't recognize it as a Call... or you don't realize what it's calling you to do.

But I'm getting ahead of myself. We're not at the Call part of the Journey yet. We are at Ordinary Life. This is where we are before we really receive the Call.

Consider two literary examples... In *The Wizard of Oz,* Dorothy's Ordinary Life is in Kansas on the farm, where things are pretty humdrum for her. Aunt Em is counting chickens. Dorothy is bored. And in *The Hobbit,* Bilbo Baggins is contentedly living an Ordinary Life in his safe little hobbit neighborhood, smoking his pipe and loving his day-to-day routine.

In reality, Ordinary Life also looks different for each person. Some people may be quite content with things as they are, while others yearn for something more.

Pamela (the author I met at my son's wedding) tells us about her Ordinary Life. She was trying to stay in the Mormon Church and remain with her husband:

> The life path for me was clearly laid out: follow the
> leaders—they know best. Faithfulness in the only true

religion on Earth was the way to happiness. I was pouring myself into everyone else, always trying to please everyone else—trying to be that person who would never be punished again, trying to be that person who would be loved by my mother, trying to be that woman who would be good enough as a wife and a mother. And at the end of the day, I was just empty and drained. There was no sense of power for me.

You truncate yourself as you continue to pretend that nothing is wrong, that your marriage is good, or you love your church, or whatever it is for you… that little piece of unexpressed "you" that is like acid on your soul, that eats away at it.

Maureen says that it was different for her. Her Ordinary Life was going well.

I landed myself on the U.S. Women's Cycling Team and was just living my dream. I absolutely loved what I did. I had two opportunities at the world championships and, in 1991, I was setting myself up just right for the Olympic Games the following year, so everything was clicking and really going well.

Lisa, like Maureen, speaks about how she was living a seeming success story in her Ordinary Life.

I built this music school and met all of the success metrics that anyone else who was looking at it from the outside would call successful. The number of students, the number of performances, the quality of how we were playing, the opportunities we were getting—it was all there.

What about You?

Do you have a sense of your Ordinary Life at the moment?

If you don't, maybe it's because you are still saying, *I'm not a Heroine! I'm not an author like Pamela, a professional athlete like Maureen, or a doctor and musician like Lisa. They're all accomplished. I'm not.*

OK, wait a minute. You are on the Heroine's Journey. You are a Heroine! Maybe it would help if I position you differently so you can see it.

Come with me.

A Mountaintop Perspective

We're all unique individuals. We are different from each other, and our lives reflect that in terms of wealth, education, geography, health, culture, looks, age and accomplishments, just to name a few! Undeniably, we women are not alike.

Yet this book invites you to discover an important similarity. To see it, you need to take a few steps back.

No, more steps back.

Farther back... away from your up-close stuck-in-the-middle-of-life view.

More.

OK, that's good.

But now you need a higher vantage point.

Start climbing.

Higher.

Picture yourself on top of a really tall mountain.

Now, use your imagination and view the landscape you see from your high perch as the landscape of your life.

There's a road down there, a path that represents where you've been.

(We're pretending. Just go with it, OK?)

Let's look more closely at that landscape. The challenges you've faced may look like dark forests or caves or rocky terrain. The happy times of your life might be grassy, sunshine-filled meadows. Your life path goes through all of it.

See it all down there? Good.

However you imagine it, just pretend that you can see it as a road through all kinds of topography. You can even go with yellow brick, if you want to. It's your life Journey, laid out perfectly, far below where you currently watch from your imagination-powered height.

This is the perspective I had in mind. You are temporarily removed from the vibrant, or maybe not-so-vibrant, center of your current life and are viewing where you've been from a distance.

Now, suppose there are other women with you on top of your mountain. Yes, they are around you. Imagine them too. They are doing the same thing, viewing their life landscapes, the paths of their own lives. They see their twists and turns, peaks and valleys, and dark passages, the dead ends of where they've been up to now... just like you.

See any similarities in those paths... things you could point to that are the same on every path?

All of us have points on our paths where our footprints disappear, where our feet leave the path and we seem to take a big jump—a Leap. Our footprints appear again, farther down the way, but often on a different path. With that Leap, we've ultimately altered not only our Journey, but also ourselves.

We women Leap. We follow our path, and when something prompts or pushes us to take a risk, make a change or do something differently... we do it! We leave the path. We Leap—or fall—into the unknown.

There are other similarities in all these women's paths. We see that every path, no matter whose it is, has twists and turns. We see that each of us has run into roadblocks and dead ends. We've all made wrong turns that took us backward, instead of forward.

Some paths have circles where we've gone round and round. We see dark chasms in all our paths.

We also see the sunlit vales and the bright meadows. We've been there too, though some have spent more time there than others. But remember, we're not judging or resenting others. You can't compare how you take the Journey to how another does, even though the Journey markers are similar.

It's good to stand up here on the mountaintop together. It's important that instead of noting and judging the differences (*Her Leap was bigger than mine!*), we see all the things we have in common. We view our path from this high vantage point so that we can see the common milestones in all our life paths. We have *all* been through them, most likely many times. For those of you who feel alone, this may be useful. Our Journey is ultimately the same, and it fits into the larger, common pattern we call the "Heroine's Journey."

As we continue observing from our mountaintop, we recognize how our Journey shapes us. Those hardships along the way make us who we are: strong, wise, resilient women. The Journey challenges us. It's hard. But what about the alternative? Would a wide, smooth, straight road produce such an awesome result as you?

Life is about experiencing these Journey steps. Joseph Campbell, referring to characters in a story, but recognizing that it's our story too, wrote it this way:

> The basic story of the hero's journey involves *giving up where you are,* going into the realm of adventure, coming to some kind of symbolically rendered realization, and then returning to the field of normal life.[1]

"Giving up where you are" is what I call "making a **Leap**." It's those Leaps that make the Journey more challenging and ultimately more meaningful for our own personal growth. Staying on the prescribed path or hanging out in our comfort zone may seem more desirable, but the Leap is what brings growth.

It's a courageous woman who Leaps. She moves into unknown territory. It can be frightening or, at the very least, uncomfortable. Women who respond to the idea/nudge/Call/push to leave the path and make the Leap are Heroines. Their trajectory is one that can be traced to, and ultimately defined as, the Heroine's Journey.

I invite you to see it is the very "her-story" of your life. You have lived and are living the Heroine's Journey.

I am a Heroine. You are a Heroine. We are together on this path, living the Heroine's Journey.

There you have it: my spiel to those of you who just can't wrap your head around calling yourself a Heroine. If you still can't, that's OK too. Just keep journeying with us. It may come with time.

Chapter 4

You Can Ignore It, but It Won't Go Away

The Call

The familiar life horizon has been outgrown; the old concepts, ideals and emotional patterns no longer fit; the time for the passing of a threshold is at hand.

—Joseph Campbell, *The Hero With a Thousand Faces*

As we go through these transitions, we go into a different territory, a deeper part of ourselves, and perhaps a very different version of ourselves. It will involve letting go of some old stories that have been outgrown. But we have to embrace those old selves as also part of our whole. It's been important for me to acknowledge that where I came from is also part of me and helped me to make that move.

—Lisa Chu, *Real-Life Heroine*

Pamela, Maureen, Lisa, you and I—all Heroines—go along living our lives in Ordinary Life, in our comfort zones, not even knowing we are in a comfort zone. Things are running along as they usually do, until something happens—there's a Call. This can be an event, a person seeking you out, an inner urging… a Call to leave Ordinary Life and enter an unknown world.

The Call happens differently for everyone and is unique in what it asks from each of us. It's designed to encourage us to do what we need to do next to grow.

Sometimes, Calls are from that still, small voice within: your intuition. You might have a gut feeling that you need to do something. It may also come as a feeling that you've outgrown where you are in your job or in a relationship. Something doesn't seem to be working for you anymore.

Or the Call can come from external circumstances. You get fired. You get offered a promotion. Someone says something that causes you to rethink a situation. Calls can come from anywhere and everywhere.

There are several different theories about where Calls come from. In his book, *Answering Your Call: A Guide for Living Your Deepest Purpose*, John P. Schuster shares some of these theories:

- For the more spiritually/theologically inclined, *"The call is God talking to you."*

- For the more psychologically inclined, *"The call is your higher self sending you a message about what you should be doing."*

- For the more biologically inclined, *"Our brain cells need stimulation or they shrivel up under the routine of life. So the call and its urges and voices are sets of neurons stretching themselves out for new stimulation, the kind that comes from new challenges."*

- For the more sociologically inclined, *"The call is the part of society and your upbringing that you have coded into your own internal messages, saying, 'Yoo hoo! Wake up and get on with your life.'"*[2]

No theory is wrong. It's whatever feels true for you.

I tend to go with the theory that the Call is God talking to you. That's also how I define an "intuitive hit." I don't feel like it's my brain coming up with something. It comes from someplace else. It's a skill in itself to learn how to be still and quiet enough to hear those deeper Calls.

How you respond to the Call is up to you. You have a choice. Yes, you even have a choice when the Call is something external that forces you out of Ordinary Life... like if you're promoted to the corporate office in another state or if you get seriously ill. *You* get to choose how to respond to all Calls.

Some people respond right away to a Call. Other people will think about it for a time, even a long time, while still others will avoid it like the plague. The latter type of response is called "Refusal of the Call" in Heroine's Journey terminology and it can go on for years. (I'm great at the Refusal.)

Timing is everything here. When and how to answer a particular Call is completely unique to each person. You might not be ready when the Call first comes around. But you also can't ignore it forever. After all, Heroines know that:

> ...things must happen when it is time for them to happen. Quests may not simply be abandoned; prophecies may not be left to rot like unpicked fruit; unicorns may go unrescued for a long time, but not forever; a happy ending cannot come in the middle of the story.[3]

Personally, whenever I've had a Call that I ignore because it's scary, or for whatever reason, it doesn't leave me alone. It keeps reappearing in my consciousness, and that tells me that I need to pay attention.

As we've seen, there are adventures that you choose to take, like discovering your career or exploring a new relationship. There are also adventures into which you are thrown, like being laid off from your job or finding out your spouse is having an affair. There's also the blunder, where you fall into an adventure unknowingly.

The famous literary Heroine Alice blundered right into her adventure when she fell down a rabbit hole. As Joseph Campbell explains to us:

> ...a blunder—apparently the merest chance—reveals an unsuspected world, and the individual is drawn into a relationship with forces that are not rightly understood... [But] blunders are not the merest chance. They are the result of suppressed desires and conflicts. They are ripples on the surface of life, produced by unsuspected springs.[4]

How did the Call manifest for our women?
Pamela's Call came unexpectedly while she was acting.

> I was cast in a play called "Extremities" as the roommate who has this big long monologue about how she was raped when she was sixteen. And what could she do? Why would she tell anyone? Everyone would know it was her fault because she'd smoked pot.
>
> I could have written that monologue. One night in rehearsal, I spoke those words, and it was not my character speaking, it was me. I came face-to-face with all those feelings I had bottled up. Those feelings that said, "You're not good enough. It's your fault." And I cried and I cried, and that was the moment for me when I realized this secret is not staying put. It was from that moment that I started healing from my own rape.
>
> The Call for me was honestly looking at and taking the lid off the secrets. Looking at my life and seeing how many secrets there really were and all those things that I was trying to pretend were OK.

Maureen's Call also was very unexpected. She was bicycling.

My vision would blur when I would ride really hard, and so I figured that I needed glasses and that I was in a bit of a poorly timed slump, because I wasn't riding as well. The women's team was going to race in France at the women's Tour de France. I was hoping that [my issues] would go away and I would get back on form. But one of the first stages of the Tour de France was a mountain stage. By the time we crested the mountain to the top, my vision blurred so severely that I lost my sight completely. I veered off the side of the road, my tires hit the gravel, my wheels came out from underneath me, and I crashed pretty badly.

I got back on my bike and completed that stage of the race, still hoping that I could continue, but I had ten stages ahead of me and my coaches had a different idea. "Maureen," they said, "if you can't see, then you need to go home." I knew I had to. I didn't want to, but I did. I went through a battery of tests and a doctor told me that I had multiple sclerosis. I was shocked.

The Call for me was "Now what do you do?" And the Call really felt like I needed to take what had happened in my life, optimize my health the best I could, and live the best life I could live.

Lisa describes her Call as, first, a feeling in her body.

I was very surprised to start feeling, in my body, in my spirit, just an exhaustion and a gradual decline in my ability to balance my work with the rest of the life that I wanted to have. And I really didn't have much of a life other than the school for most of those years. But the reason it was surprising was, you know, hey... I chose this. I created it. How could it possibly be depleting me? It's the thing I went out on a limb to do, and that made the acknowledgment of what I was feeling that much more difficult. First, the decision was a feeling in my body that I really needed to take some time off.

It didn't come to me as a plan. I did allow it to go on for quite a while as I was sorting it all out. I was taking all these small steps for myself, creating more space in my life. Then I was agonizing over decisions, asking myself, "What do I want to do?" And then finally, there was a moment when I knew. I just knew what I needed to do.

The Call was so different for each of them.

- Pamela burst into tears when the script she was reading matched with a traumatic event in her life. She realized her secrets couldn't stay put.

- Maureen's cycling career came to an abrupt halt with a shocking diagnosis. She had to figure out where to go from there.

- Lisa got a feeling in her body that spoke to her about how she was living her life. She couldn't continue living the depleting life she had chosen.

But there was also one significant similarity, and it's the same for everyone. The Call arrives with this general message for all of us. *You know how things have been going? Well, you need to grow, so it's time for a change!*

One of my favorite personal Calls came prior to the start of my second marriage. I had been divorced for about three years. Ordinary Life was good. About that time, I went on a business trip with this really nice guy. We had a fun time, but I knew he had a live-in girlfriend. I thought that maybe a spark had been lit, but I had no plans to do anything about it. One cold Maine night, I was out walking my dog, and the Call came crashing in on my quiet reverie. *Call him!*

This wasn't blundering into anything. This was a direct do-it-now thought planting itself within me! Surprisingly for me, a practiced Call-refuser, I didn't refuse this Call.

Was I anxious? Yes, very. The Threshold Guardians screamed their dire warnings at me. *He'll spurn you! He's got a girlfriend. They're probably engaged. You have two children! What are you thinking?* And on and on. The warnings were unceasing, but I persevered.

The next day, during lunch, I picked up my phone.

"Hi, Robin. This is Susanna." (Some inconsequential small talk...) "I'm calling to see if you want to go out to lunch with me."

Silence. (The Threshold Guardians gathered around, preparing for their big *I told you so* moment!)

"That's very flattering, Susanna. Yes, I'd like that."

And with that, I stepped into a new adventure.

Eight months later, he asked me to marry him. That was over twenty-seven years ago.

Don't get me wrong. Answering the Call doesn't always happen that quickly. Yes, Heroines sometimes—oftentimes—Refuse the Call. We hear a tiny inner voice; we get an idea. And it doesn't feel comfortable, so we dismiss it. The voice gets louder; the idea gets stronger. Now it's a nudge. If it's still something we don't want to look at or deal with, we shove it into the back corner of our psyche. We ignore it. And again, we might not even see the connection of that "message" to our greater growth and betterment!

In his book, *The Journey of the Hero: Personal Growth, Deep Ecology and the Quest for the Grail*, Friedemann Wieland speaks of the origins of our Calls as "gods"—those parts of us that we suppress, bury and forget about but that want to be alive and free. He describes the peril we face if we continue to ignore them.

> In symbolic form [the uninvited gods] represent essential forces and impulses that we suppress... the parts

of ourselves that we send into exile... If we turn away and oppose these forces of life, we... push them deep into the unconscious. From here, these gods have a great deal of power. To realize themselves in human consciousness, these gods will knock, in the shape of crises, at the door of our awareness.[5]

Like many other Heroines, Maureen also had a Refusal of the Call. She tells us it took her some time to finally respond to her Call once she had been diagnosed with MS.

It took one and a half years for the Call to sink in, because I was definitely devastated and confused for some time. I needed some help to hear it. What I was doing that *wasn't* working was looking backward. I kept asking myself, "Why me? How do I fix this? How do I get my life back?"

But just wanting quick answers wasn't getting me anywhere.

The Call comes from some part of you—your soul, your intuition, your gut, your suppressed self. Some might say the Universe, Spirit, God... *something* gives you a message, a message that is meant for you alone and is pertinent, or rather *vital*, to your growth as a human being.

In his book, *Answering Your Call,* John P. Schuster writes about the Danish philosopher and theologian Søren Kierkegaard's explanation for why it's tempting to refuse Calls:

Kierkegaard had a phrase for the soul-dread we experience when the calls we'd rather not face become crystal clear. He described responding to these calls as an encounter with "fear and trembling..." If we say yes in response to these calls we overcome the fear and trembling, or at least we get used to them.[6]

Are you experiencing some of the "soul-dread" Schuster writes about? Looking back over the Leaps I've made in the past, most of them received certain amount of Refusal of the Call before I finally made the Leap.

My strongest urge to Refuse the Call was in relation to my first marriage. It took me years to accept the Call that I had to do something about the failing relationship. My practiced delay tactic was telling myself, *It will get better when...* and then I would wait for the "when"—a new addition to the house, a move, a new job. But it didn't get better. The "gods" upped the ante, the knocking got louder, and eventually, with great trepidation, I took action... but in small steps. I started seeing a therapist. That step gave me the courage to seek out a lawyer, and slowly that particular Heroine's Journey unfolded, birthing me into a very different person.

In addition to those of you who might be Refusing the Call, there are some of you who are reading this and saying, *I'm perfectly happy where I'm at right now—in my comfort zone. What's wrong with that?* Absolutely nothing! There are definitely times when we don't experience Calls. We're where we need to be for the moment. And that's fine, as long as you're honest with yourself!

What about You?

Are you getting a Call now? Any urges, demands, nudges? Are you Refusing the Call? If so, what's making you refuse it? Can you hear the knocking?

Chapter 5

You've Got Company!

Guardians of the Journey

The hero goes forward in his adventure until he comes to the "threshold guardian[s]" at the entrance to the zone of magnified power. Beyond them is darkness, the unknown and danger; just as beyond the parental watch is danger to the infant and beyond the protection of his society danger to the members of the tribe. The usual person is more than content, he is even proud, to remain within the indicated bounds, and popular belief gives him every reason to fear so much as the first step into the unexplored.

— Joseph Campbell, *The Hero With a Thousand Faces*

When you make changes, there are always going to be people who you leave behind… because there are some people who are too threatened by the changes you are making or just can't agree with what you are doing, or get angry about it… This can make it tempting to stay put and not listen to that inner voice.

— Lisa Chu, *Real-Life Heroine*

Y ou will encounter all kinds of people and hear all sorts of voices on your Journey. Some will be helpful and supportive. These are helpers, or "Mentors." Others will be the opposite, instilling fear, dread and doubt in you. They are called "Threshold Guardians."

Mentors

Mentors provide support in a multitude of ways. Maybe they offer you a safe place to stay, or they encourage your efforts. Or they give you a sign or message that helps guide you on your way. Their words are comforting. *Stay with us while you're contemplating what to do. I know you can do this. Leaving him or her will allow you to finally be yourself! Here, I wore this bracelet while going through a hard time and it comforted me.*

In fairy tales, Mentors are often disguised as something else: mice, dwarves, a scarecrow and so forth. The mice in Disney's *Cinderella* help Cinderella make it to the royal ball, the seven dwarfs help Snow White survive in the woods, and the scarecrow ends up being a trusted friend to Dorothy in Oz. Other storybook characters pass these creatures by and don't receive their help. But Heroines, like Cinderella, Snow White and Dorothy, see beyond the Mentor's facade and usually reap some kind of benefit as a result.

In real life, you probably won't meet talking mice, woodland dwarfs or a scarecrow, but you might have a tendency to ignore the wisdom of a person who has a message you need to hear. A Mentor could be your next-door neighbor, your grandmother or your workout partner. The important thing to remember is that guidance for your Journey can come from a variety of sources, and sometimes it may come from the person you least expect.

Mentors can also appear at critical moments on your path. Do you remember the Cheshire Cat in *Alice in Wonderland* appearing on a branch overhead when Alice was wondering which way to go? Several years ago, I was at a similar point in my own life, trying to decide whether to accept an offer to join a consulting firm or continue working for myself. I happened to be having lunch with a colleague, and although I didn't know her very well,

I decided to run my decision-making quandary by her. She wound up giving me the best advice. "Susanna," she asked, "do you know the adage about the man stuck on a rooftop in a flood?" I didn't, so she told it to me.

A fellow was stuck on his rooftop in a flood. He was praying to God for help.

Soon, a man in a rowboat came by, and the fellow shouted to the man on the roof, "Jump in! I can save you."

The stranded fellow shouted back, "No, it's OK, I'm praying to God, and he is going to save me."

So, the rowboat went on.

Then a motorboat came by. The motorboat captain shouted, "Jump in, I can save you."

To this, the stranded man said, "No thanks, I'm praying to God and he is going to save me. I have faith."

So, the motorboat went on.

Then a helicopter came by, and the pilot shouted down, "Grab this rope, and I will lift you to safety."

To this, the stranded man again replied, "No thanks, I'm praying to God, and he is going to save me. I have faith."

So, the helicopter reluctantly flew away.

Soon, the water rose above the rooftop and the man drowned. He went to Heaven. He finally got his chance to discuss this whole situation with God, at which point he exclaimed, "I had faith in you but you didn't save me, you let me drown. I don't understand why!"

To this, God replied, "I sent you a rowboat and a motorboat and a helicopter. What more did you expect?"

Of course, my colleague was suggesting that the man on the rooftop was me and that I had been offered a lifeline, an opportunity to get "off the roof" and join the consulting firm. Her advice led me to take a Leap and accept the firm's offer.

My story illustrates how Mentors come in many guises. They can be difficult to recognize, so be on the lookout!

Threshold Guardians

The less supportive and less positive type of guardians that you will surely meet on your Journey are the Threshold Guardians. As their name implies, Threshold Guardians become particularly overbearing around the Threshold Crossing, although they start yammering as early as the receipt of your Call. But, unfortunately, I've found that they don't always leave you alone once you Cross the Threshold. Rather, they often accompany you for much of the Journey.

Here's the thing about Threshold Guardians: I believe they mean well. Their charge is to protect you, to guard you against the dangers that lurk outside your comfort zone. They stand for the "limits of the known world," as Campbell writes. Everything outside is *dangerous!* They say things like, *You want to do what? Are you crazy? If you leave your job, you'll lose all your security.*

Threshold Guardians can be real people (for example, your parents, siblings or best friend). They can also be those negative voices in your head, sometimes called "the inner critic." Those voices can be particularly rancorous at the start of a Journey.

When I've talked with women in my workshops, I have found that everyone's inner Threshold Guardians seem to say similar things to them as they contemplate responding to a Call. It's as though there's only one script, and it sounds like this:

- I will look like a failure, a loser.
- I will feel foolish.
- I will be alone.

- I won't be strong enough.
- It will be too difficult.
- I will fail.
- I don't know how.
- I don't have enough money.
- My expectations are too high.
- What if I'm not good at it?
- What if people get angry with me or hate me?
- What if my reputation is shot?
- Nothing will come of it.
- It's too big a time commitment.
- I should be doing more productive things.

I'll bet some of these thoughts are as familiar to you as they are to me.

How do you deal with these inner voices that can freeze you and send you right back to the limits and comforts of Ordinary Life?

Being aware of them is the first step. The next step is knowing that you can choose to change these seeming "words of advice" into what *you* want. One of the Heroines in my workshop, upon hearing this, said, "Oh, I thought we were supposed to do what they said!"

Often these are old voices from your childhood—maybe the voices of your parents or other adults. We hear them when we're little, we internalize them, and then when we're adults, we think they're our own thoughts. But guess what? They aren't if you don't want them to be!

But how to dispel those voices?

This is when it is important to come up with affirmations to turn the negatives around. Here are some examples. Try saying these to yourself. Better yet, write them down and add your own!

- What I want is possible.
- I have enough. I know enough. I am enough.
- What I have is unique and special to share.
- I am reflecting the Divine Source.
- I do not have to give up my dream.
- I have what it takes.
- I will not fail. In fact, I will succeed.
- I am unique. People who know me admire me.
- I deserve better.
- I am allowed to try new things. I can spread my wings!
- It's OK to make mistakes. Making mistakes helps me become a wiser person.
- I can succeed at anything if I put my mind to it.
- I won't give up. I can do it!
- I can count on my Spirit to guide me.

Which beliefs about yourself do you want to let go of, and which ones do you want to affirm so that they guide your Journey in a positive direction?

If you look at your life and what happens to you through the framework of the Heroine's Journey, then your perceptions and reactions are more positive than if you were to look at the same things as disconnected and not part of a larger life view. Note the difference in reactions below:

Your Negative Inner Voice	Your Inner Heroine Affirmation
Yikes, this is a catastrophe!	Great! A new adventure. Let's go!
I'm a failure, not worthy. I don't have what it takes. That's for other people.	I am a Heroine. I have what it takes. I've done this before. I'm up for it.
I wouldn't want to appear conceited. I don't want the spotlight on me.	I'm unique—one of a kind. If I don't fully express myself, then the world will miss out. I let my light shine.
Oh, no! I failed! I'm done for. I've made a mistake. I can't make mistakes and be a success.	That didn't work. I made a mistake. What can I learn from this, given that it's part of what's shaping me into my fully realized self?
I'm afraid. I can't do it.	I'm ready for anything. I can handle it.
I love my comfort zone—what I know. Don't make me leave! What I don't know scares me.	With a little time, new things will soon become familiar.
They don't like me or want me.	This is not about me. I'm not taking this in, nor taking it personally. I always have a choice about what I take in and what I don't.
I'm staying put where I'm safe and comfortable.	I'm moving forward.

Your Negative Inner Voice	Your Inner Heroine Affirmation
I build walls so I don't get hurt. I don't open up in case I might get hurt.	I open myself up and allow myself to be vulnerable, and sometimes I get hurt. I recognize this as part of the Journey, part of my growth.
I only listen to the advice of others.	I trust myself. I believe in my judgment.
I have a good brain and can figure things out without listening to an "inner voice" or intuition.	I use my intuition, powers of discernment and ability to notice things to help me on my Journey, in partnership with my good brain.
I'm stuck, frustrated, worried. I'm in a bad place.	I'm unsure where to go next, but this is common on the Journey. It will become clear.
Help! This is awful. This is the worst thing that could possibly happen. I'm done for! I need to run, escape. I'm ashamed.	This must be so hard because it has to do with a Dragon, some great fear of mine. If I delve into it and understand what's frightening me, then I can move through it.
Life is hard, a struggle.	Life is an adventure. Opportunities can be disguised as troubles, calamities. I have to see them for what they really are, necessary parts of the Journey that will help me develop into my full self!

As you can see, Heroines have a different mindset overall, a different way of approaching things and looking at the world. When you see the world and life as a vehicle for your own growth, then even a calamity can become a potential gift. It's not being a Pollyanna. It's knowing that things aren't always as they seem, as reflected in the Taoist fable *Maybe:*

> There was an old farmer who had worked his crops for many years. One day his horse ran away. Upon hearing the news, his neighbors came to visit.
>
> "Such bad luck," they said sympathetically.
>
> "Maybe," the farmer replied.
>
> The next morning the horse returned, bringing with it three wild horses.
>
> "How wonderful," the neighbors exclaimed.
>
> "Maybe," replied the old man.
>
> The following day, his son tried to ride one of the untamed horses, was thrown, and broke his leg. The neighbors came again to offer their sympathy on his misfortune.
>
> "Maybe," answered the farmer.
>
> The day after, military officials came to the village to draft young men into the army. Seeing that the son's leg was broken, they passed him by. The neighbors congratulated the farmer on how well things had turned out.
>
> "Maybe," said the farmer.

If you see the full expanse of the Heroine's Journey, then you don't necessarily make a judgment about any particular event. It remains to be seen how it will contribute to your betterment, to your Journey. Heroines take everything as it comes, without judging it good or bad.

And as you contemplate a Call, as you stand at the Threshold of a new adventure, are you hearing the Threshold Guardian voices? Write down their warnings—every last one. Then, write your Heroine's affirmations. Tell the voices what's really true for *you*. Because *you* know. They don't. They are just reading off an old script.

In *The Croods*, an animated movie about a caveman family, the dad believes that no one should leave the safety of the cave. That's what he was taught. But he is living from an old script. Now times have changed. The family needs to go out into the world in order to survive. He keeps resisting change (Refusing the Call) until circumstances force him to see it differently.[7]

Calls ask you to get out of the cave! The Threshold Guardians might think the saber-toothed tiger is right around the corner. He isn't. It's your bright future.

And as you work to block out the cries of the Threshold Guardians, don't forget to listen for the wise words of your Mentors. Sometimes, it's hard to hear them above the din of everything else. But hearing them and knowing that there are others who will help you can give you the much-needed strength to keep moving forward on your Journey.

Chapter 6

Close Your Eyes and Plug Your Nose!

The Leap

The original departure into the land of trials represent[s] only the beginning of the long and really perilous path of initiatory conquests and moments of illumination. Dragons have now to be slain and surprising barriers passed—again, again and again. Meanwhile there will be a multitude of preliminary victories, unretainable ecstasies and momentary glimpses of the wonderful land.

> — Joseph Campbell, *Hero With A Thousand Faces*

That summer, I had just gotten divorced and I was sitting out on my deck looking out on my yard and I thought, "My yard looks like crap." In my head, I started with the excuses: but my mower's broken, I don't have a sprinkler system and those trees are dead. I heard my father's voice saying, "That's an excuse. What's the reason?" I stopped and thought, *Well, the reasons are I don't water, I don't mow, and I don't have a chainsaw.* That weekend I went out and I bought a chainsaw, got my mower fixed, and in a couple of months had my sprinkler system fixed. It was such a metaphor for me because as I took control of my yard, I began to take more control of my life. There is no power in the excuse. There is power in doing what you can control. That's where the power is.

> — Pamela McCreary, *Real-Life Heroine*

This is the point in your Heroine's Journey when you've heard your Call and you're ready to respond. You've committed to following through on whatever it is that your nudge, intuition or call-to-action is asking of you. What happens next?

Now it's time for the big action step in your Heroine's Journey, Crossing the Threshold. It's so big a step that I like to call it a Leap. The actual Leap part of the Heroine's Journey is the Crossing the Threshold milestone. It's when you hold your nose and jump…

…into the unknown, to begin your adventure.

You don't feel comfortable? Of course, you don't! You've left your comfort zone behind.

What was Pamela's Leap? She left her church and her marriage in order to free her traumatic secrets.

Maureen's Leap? She made a powerful decision to stop looking back at her life before MS and to instead look forward in her life to what she could do now.

Lisa's Leap? She closed her music school.

What about You?

Are you contemplating a Leap? Are you mid-Leap? Are you just landing after your Leap?

As you consider whether you're pre-, mid- or post-Leap, it's important to notice that a Leap has distinct parts to it, parts that may or may not happen in this order:

- *Preparing* (Getting ready and gathering your courage)
- *Mourning* (Feeling the loss of what you're leaving behind)
- *Leaping* (Taking action with a first step)
- Sometimes… *Reversing the Action* ("I'd rather not do this. I'm not ready.")
- *Mid-Leap* (feeling panic, excitement, fear… "What have I done? I'm ungrounded!")
- *Landing* (You're on the road again… but now what?)

One of the most common and intense feelings during a Leap is fear (or a similar emotion like anxiety, worry or doubt). It's not a comfortable emotion. But it's important to remember that it's a constant companion of every Heroine.

Fear will be there during each of the distinct parts of the Leap, and beyond. I advise Heroines to make friends with their fear and learn to manage it. It's a given that you'll experience it on the Journey. That being said, I do believe that the more you respond to your inner Calls (your intuition), the stronger that intuition gets and the more you can trust it. That helps counteract fear.

Another bit of counsel I offer is to remember that Leaps are different for everyone. What is scary for you might not be scary for me, and vice versa. Courage is courage. Never judge another Heroine's Leap!

Yes, Leaping can be frightening. But you can get used to making big Leaps by practicing smaller, less significant Leaps. Think of Leaping as a muscle you can strengthen. And you can strengthen it by finding different ways to leave your comfort zone and trying out new things.

Of course, I have the perfect Task for this.

Task Three: The Comfort Zone Challenge

Let me begin by clarifying that "comfort zone" should technically be in the plural (comfort zones) since you have many… in all the separate areas of your life.

- You have a creativity comfort zone that has you saying, *Oh, I'm not an artist. I'm not creative. I can't paint.* If you find yourself using the word "can't," then most likely you're operating inside of a comfort zone.

- You have a physical fitness comfort zone where you can be heard remarking, *I don't dance. I look ridiculous.* Or, *I'm not in good enough shape to take that workout class.*

- You have a social-circle comfort zone where you say, *I can't say what I really think. People will think I'm rude. They won't like me.*

- You have comfort zones around meeting people, learning new things, traveling, eating… Comfort zones exist in all areas of your life.

My challenge for you is to choose one or two of your comfort zones and then identify what would constitute a mini-Leap outside of each one. Remember, this is a mini-Leap as defined by *you,* not by anyone else.

If it's the creativity comfort zone, then maybe you try a painting or a drawing class. Or start smaller and buy a coloring book.

If it's the physical fitness comfort zone, then maybe you take a dance class or sign up for a week or two at a gym.

If it's the social comfort zone, commit to voicing your opinion when you'd normally stay quiet or go with the flow. For instance, maybe when a friend suggests meeting for dinner at a restaurant you don't like, be honest about not liking that restaurant and then suggest a different place to eat.

I've challenged clients in this way, and their comfort zone Leaps have been varied.

- One woman resolved to tell her mother something she had held back for years.

- One woman decided to do something creative every Wednesday.

- One woman who didn't like to cook decided to try a new recipe every week.

The practice Leap can be something very small. Maybe you've never walked into a store that you've been interested in because it seems too snooty and you're afraid of being judged, but you make the Leap and go in. You may or may not like what you find, but you've exercised your Leapability. You can do it. You're sending yourself a message that you're willing to leave that zone of comfort when it's right for you.

List at least three ways that you will stretch beyond your Comfort Zone by _____ (fill in the date).

I will	The fears this brings up are	What I'm saying to my fears

Like I said before, Leaping is a muscle that you can strengthen. It's the leaving-your-comfort-zone muscle that gets you to try something you haven't before. You'll see that you expand as a result. You'll realize that you survive it. You'll do things that you won't want to repeat, but you'll have a better sense of what you *do* want to do again.

It's fine to do this exercise by yourself, but I've found that it's even better if you can find some friends to do it with you. They'll help keep you motivated... and honest. Get together and decide on what you'll do, then meet again at a set date, and report how it went.

Go ahead. I challenge you! Be uncomfortable! Leave that Comfort Zone!

Chapter 7

Expect the Unexpected

The Road of Adventure

The belly is the dark place where digestion takes place and new energy is created. The story of Jonah in the whale is an example of a mythic theme that is practically universal, of the hero going into a fish's belly and ultimately coming out again, transformed.

— Joseph Campbell, *Power Of Myth*

Outside of your comfort zone lie the dragons, the self-doubts, the concerns. And if you can't motivate yourself with self-compassion, then it's going to be a miserable journey. It's going to be a painful journey if we're beating ourselves up—if we want to go crawling back into our comfort zones, saying things like, "I didn't really want to do that. That wasn't that fun." Well, maybe it wasn't fun because you made it hell. Compassion is vital.

— Maureen Manley, *Real-Life Heroine*

You've Leaped, you've landed, you've caught your breath… you look around. Where are you? You're on the **Road of Adventure**, that's where!

Once on the Road, all kinds of things happen. Some of them are difficult, and some of them are pretty nice, but they're all valuable and useful, if you can see them in the right light. People show up, just like they did when you were contemplating your Call. Some of them, your Mentors, want to help you. Other people, sometimes even your own inner voices, are not helpful. They are the Threshold Guardians.

But all the challenges are there to help you learn whatever it is you need to learn on this particular Journey. You have to pass through this vale of tears, this Belly of the Whale, to be reborn, find peace and become a stronger, more fulfilled version of yourself.

I want you to take a look at what happened to our Heroines while they were on their adventures. Lots happened, of course, but here's a sampling.

Pamela tells us that she learned to give others what she wanted to receive.

> It wasn't like I left the church and it was all sweetness
> and light. I left the Mormon Church that my mother
> had joined when I was a young girl. It was an insti-
> tution that gave her boundaries and the sense that she
> was loved and safe. It created a safety net for my mom,
> but I didn't need that. I needed a different net. I had
> to go outside that church to find my path.
>
> My mother was furious. I spent so much time,
> again, trying to be good enough so that she would
> love me. None of it made a difference until I realized
> that I was being as judgmental of her as I thought she
> was being of me. I was judging her for staying. I was
> angry with her for staying. It was about making her
> wrong, and she was telling me that I was wrong for
> leaving.
>
> When I realized that I was judging her, I didn't
> want to do that. This was her choice. It wasn't until

I gave her that thing I was expecting from her that I actually got it in return. Once I was able to accept her for who she was, I got the same thing in return.

Maureen tells us about how she learned to leave the past behind and to "live forward."

Because of the MS, my vision was very bad... it would blur even when I wasn't exercising, and I was walking with a cane at the time. But I was trying to live my life forward. I was really thinking, practicing and focusing on what I could see. But it was still a constant challenge.

One day, I drove to the lake in my town to sit by the water. I was having an OK day, so I left my cane in the car and walked down to the lakeside. As I walked, my body temperature increased and my legs started to feel very unstable and wobbly beneath me. Then, as I walked farther, my body temperature went even higher, and that's when my vision began to blur.

When I reached the edge of the lake, I sat on a park bench to rest, and as I looked out across Lake Washington, I couldn't see the other side, which is Seattle. It was all a big blur. I became overwhelmed with what had happened in my life and all that I had lost. I was sitting there feeling miserable, with my legs wobbling and my vision failing, and then a thought came to me that was so powerful that I truly don't know if I thought it or if it thought me. *Focus on what you can see and not on what you can't.*

That thought snapped me into the present moment, where I returned to my practice of living my life forward—of looking at what I *can* do and working with that.

Sitting there on the bench, I brought my vision in closer to where I could see just fine. It was only when I looked out far that my vision got blurry. So, focusing on what wasn't blurry, I could see the park bench that I was sitting on. I could see Lake Washington's water lapping up against the shore. As I rested there, my body temperature came down, my vision cleared up and my legs felt better.

I knew that I wouldn't be able to walk down the road, but I knew I could walk to the next bench. I had a choice: I could sit and feel sorry for myself, or I could move and do what I could, without knowing the outcome. I chose to get up and walk to the next bench, where I rested, and then I got up and walked to the next bench and rested again.

That truly was a threshold experience that would launch me into the rest of my life.

Lisa tells us about letting go of teaching music and, by doing so, discovering the music inside.

Once I no longer had the violin school, it became about finding the music within. My love of music has been with me since I was three years old, probably before. That love drew me to the process of improvisation and the principles behind it, which are listening, offering and being in the moment. It drew me to playing without a script, which for me is hugely outside of my comfort zone because all the music I've ever played has been written down.

For the first time, I started playing without any written music, without anyone telling me what to do. No one knew how it was supposed to go because it was new. The music I played had never been done before. I love that as a metaphor for what we are facing in our society. Often there isn't a script, so we don't know what's next. How do we become comfortable in that zone where we're flying by the seat of our pants? I've been playing that out literally, doing music improvisation.

I believe that inside us, there is a deep knowing. We are born with an essence that is longing to come out, and it's urging us in small ways throughout our lives. It's about us having the ability to be still, make the space, create the silence, and to listen to that. That is difficult to do with all the stimuli from the world and the messages we get from the outside.

I have been getting out of the way more and more, and much has emerged as a result. I've found there's so much there that I could never have planned or imagined myself. You can hear that in my music. I'm blossoming, and what's happened to me is representative of what happens when we let go.

There's another one of my Leaps that I'd like to share with you, because it illustrates how things on the Road of Adventure can be very unpredictable.

My close colleague, Brenda, and I worked together in the manufacturing company where I had been employed for twelve years. We did a lot together, both inside the company and also while facilitating for organizations outside the firm. One late afternoon, our director called us both into her office and told us that the project we had worked on together for the past year was being "back-burnered." We were devastated. I personally had spent hours learning new technology just to do this project. I'd put in late hours but had been excited about the possibilities the project could bring to the company. And now... nothing would happen. We knew how it usually worked. Once something was shelved, it never got brought forward again. We knew about the force of OBE, being "overcome by events."

That day, Brenda and I left the office, but before going home, we sat down in a vacant conference room to complain to each other. We let it rip. We were frustrated, angry, tired, disappointed. And so, we vented.

"Isn't that always the way?"

"They don't know what they're doing at the top. They follow one thing, then another."

"We're the pawns of whatever they fancy in the moment."

Blah, blah, blah... Complain, complain, complain... We kept spewing negativity, which felt perfectly OK because that's what people are used to doing. It's bonding in a negative, downer sort of way. Let's get together and share what we hate in common.

Then, I had one of those sudden intuition "drop-ins," the kind that feels like it comes from a force outside yourself. I had the clear knowledge that I had to stop the negativity I was putting out there and instead share what I *wanted* to happen.

It was evident to me that this negative diatribe was a useless exercise.

"This is wasted energy," I said to Brenda.

We were spending good energy dwelling on what we didn't want. Where does that get you? More of the same, and I certainly didn't want that.

Immediately, Brenda was right there with me. Only a few weeks prior, we had been helping some interns envision how they wanted their year to go. Well, the two of us could do the same. What did we really want to be doing? We needed to get clear on that and put our energy *there* instead of putting it into what we didn't want!

For the next year, we met together and planned until we had a map of what needed to happen... a Leap. This one was big— leaving the company and starting our own business! But we did it.

We became a facilitation company of two, providing our services to companies and nonprofits.

This was a big move for both of us. I had been at the company for twelve years and Brenda for longer. Neither of us had ever been in business for ourselves. Yes, we knew about planning and we did a lot of it. But marketing? I knew nothing about it. Bookkeeping? Nope. Writing proposals? Ugh. All of it was new, and the road ahead was daunting. Yes, we had Crossed the Threshold and could feel the winds of freedom, and they felt good, but… it was scary on the Road. Would we be able to find clients? It was a heady and anxiety-inducing time. (By the way, you may have noted that this was not a solo Leap. That happens. Sometimes you have a Threshold where you really lean on someone for support. If I'm completely honest with myself, I don't think I would have attempted it on my own. I was leaning on Brenda more than I realized at the time that we leaped. But that was to be amended, as you'll soon see.)

So, there we were, an excited and anxious duo wondering how we were going to make it. Then, an unexpected windfall occurred. Contract negotiations were to begin at our now-former company. This was the first time management and the union would be collaborating, using a joint management/union team to negotiate. Because Brenda and I had been pivotal in training this negotiating team while we were still at the company, we were offered consulting jobs as facilitators for the negotiations.

This was huge! This was just the kind of work the two of us had envisioned. They were hiring us back as consultants! Talk about "Leap and the net will appear!"

It was a life-changing experience for me, working with those men to negotiate a new contract. They didn't merely want a revision to the old contract. No, they wanted a totally new way of working together. They wanted to be more efficient, more competitive—they wanted to become a high-powered working organization. To say this was a complex challenge for this team of men (six union and six management) is a vast understatement. We worked through a hot summer in a classroom with no air conditioning. The large union labor force of over eight thousand was kept apprised of what was happening, and they were often in an uproar about the changes being proposed. Sometimes our team would have to placate an unruly crowd during the process.

In spite of the odds, the team did it. They brought it all together, and the union voted it in. The accomplishment was huge! They did it together and devised a new way of working with each other. The accolades were equally huge. The head of the international union came more than once to congratulate them. Then, on Labor Day, 1994, President Bill Clinton came to speak to the company and praise their groundbreaking effort.

Wow! What a way to launch a business! Brenda and I were on our way!

Well, not quite.

After the high pinnacle of the contract negotiations, our work became non-existent. Maybe we had a couple of clients, but after some good money coming our way during the summer, the fall was very lean.

That gave us time… time to meet, time to do more planning, but also time to realize we had very different styles of working. We hadn't had the opportunity to see this before. We began to think maybe this was why people always said to be careful about partnerships. They're tough. We had a hard time agreeing on how to go about everything. Finally, Brenda sat me down and told me she didn't want to continue working with me. It was a hard but courageous thing for her to say.

Looking back, I'm glad we went our separate ways. In the long run, it helped me. But at the time, it felt awful. Brenda didn't want me. I felt rejected. We—or rather, I—had failed. I didn't know how to work without her. What was I going to do?

Remember me telling you about the Belly of the Whale—that time after your Leap when you often have all kinds of false starts, setbacks, failures and successes? Well, this was it for me… in living color!

When you're in the Belly of the Whale, you're churned around and everything is chaotic and uncertain. What you thought would happen doesn't. What was reality before is now totally different. I'm sure that we need to experience these times of struggle in order for us to grow. But it's hard to remember that when you're getting tossed about!

Back then I didn't say to myself, *Susanna, you're just going through a metaphorical rebirth*. But that's exactly what was happening.

When I came through my deep despair, I knew I had to keep going somehow.

I knew that even though I thought I couldn't do it alone, I had to make it work. I needed the money, and I didn't want to lose face even more.

So, I did the bootstraps thing and pulled myself up. I wrote proposals. I winged what I didn't know. I got jobs, and I learned and learned. I did well and helped people. Slowly, I made it on my own and made a name for myself in the process.

And I grew tremendously, both in my concept of who I was and in what I could do. I had stretched considerably, and as painful as it was, I was grateful for the remarkable outcome.

What about You?

You're on your own version of the yellow brick road. Have you Crossed the Threshold? Braved the Threshold Guardians? Maybe you've achieved the leaving-your-comfort-zone part and faced all the loss and terror associated with that. Have you left behind whatever was important for you to leave behind? Now you're out on the Road, working through the messiness of life. That's the Heroine's Journey. There are ups and downs.

Throughout it all, I hope you're not complaining and moaning… focusing on what you *don't* want. Instead, I hope you're focusing on what you *do* want, like Brenda and I finally did in the conference room.

This is a good time for me to share a tool that will help you focus your thoughts on what you want. I call it "Doing a Circle."[8] It's simple.

Find a blank sheet of paper and draw a big circle on it. Starting on the outside of that circle, write down those negative thoughts of yours, the things you don't want. For example, if it's about your job, what are the things you *don't* want in a job? You might write as follows:

- A micromanaging boss
- Unfriendly coworkers
- A long commute to the office
- Work that is meaningless

You get the idea. I call this the *Is Not* list. It's what you're *not* looking for in a job.

Remarkably, when people are in a job that is full of the things they don't want, they dwell on those things. And then they're surprised when that's what continues to come their way.

On the inside of the circle, write down what you *do* want (in a job, for instance). This is called the *Is* list. Often, you can start with the reverse of the Is Not list:

- A boss who trusts me
- Friendly coworkers
- An easy and short commute
- Meaningful work

List everything that you'd like (in a job or whatever it is you're wanting to be different in your life). But be aware. There are three snags to look for when you're Doing a Circle.

- Only write what you want for *you*, not what you want for someone else. Meaning, you can't write *Joe likes me*. Or *My son is an A student*. That's *their* circle, not yours.

- Negatives can easily sneak into your *Is* list. Only write things that are worded positively. So instead of writing that you are injury-free, you'd write that you are strong and healthy. Even though injury-free is what you want, it's still a focus on the negative (injury) rather than the positive (healthy).

- Let go of how your *Is* list might show up for you. Essentially, you have to think of the universe as a drive-thru window where you're "placing your order" by writing it inside the circle. Then, let the universe take care of your order. Don't try to figure out how it will happen. Just have faith that it will, and then go about your business.

When you're finished writing, put your paper somewhere where you can see it, so it can remind you that you want to focus on what's inside the circle. Keep your thoughts there.

Doing a Circle is a tool for envisioning what you want. I've used it successfully for finding, uncovering or manifesting what I'm looking for: a new home, a new job, a new lover, a new associate and so on.

To give your vision even more power, it helps to feel or put yourself into the feeling place of what you're visioning. Meaning that if you were in a job that had those things you've put in your circle, how would you feel? Let yourself really *feel* those emotions. Your thoughts, words and feelings have power. This is an exercise that helps you put them all together in a very focused way.

So, when you find yourself stuck, dwelling on what isn't working... *Stop!* Do a Circle!

Now, let's return to the Road of Adventure. What has happened or is happening to you on the Road? Your comfort zone is behind you. How have you grown, and how have you changed? Have you let go of something, someone or some way of being that no longer fits the person you're becoming?

Maybe you're wondering which way to go next. If so, the next chapter might offer some assistance. Read on to learn of another tool that will help you chart your course while on your Heroine's Journey.

Chapter 8

You Own the Perfect Compass

Mapping Your Course

Bill Moyers: Do you ever have this sense when you are following your bliss, as I have at moments, of being helped by hidden hands?

Joseph Campbell: All the time. It is miraculous. I even have a superstition that has grown on me as the result of invisible hands coming all the time—namely, that if you do follow your bliss, you put yourself on a kind of track that has been there all the while, waiting for you, and the life that you ought to be living is the one you are living. When you can see that, you begin to meet people who are in the field of your bliss, and they open the doors to you. I say, follow your bliss and don't be afraid, and doors will open where you didn't know they were going to be.

— Joseph Campbell, *The Power Of Myth*

You're on the Road of Adventure. It's fun. It's exciting. It's frightening. It's confusing! Maybe you're at that point where you're not sure where to go or which way is best. Luckily, there's another task that Heroines can do that can be a useful tool for this point in your Journey. But before I share it, I'll first give you a little background information about it... because developing the process was part of my own Road of Adventure on a previous Heroine's Journey.

During my time at the manufacturing company, I learned a group process—a form of structured brainstorming. I used this process to facilitate problem-solving, to envision the future, to develop project plans, and to brainstorm. I kept tweaking it and, eventually, I used it exclusively as a means to help groups develop long-term strategic plans. When I left the company and went out on my own, I continued to use the process to help schools, boards of directors, companies and nonprofits devise strategic plans.

Each participant submitted ideas in response to one question: "Given ideal circumstances, what will my organization look like, be like or be doing three years from now?"

From these ideas came the goals that the participants, as a group, would focus on within their organization over the next three years.

At some point, the idea came to me to use this same strategic planning process with individuals. I asked myself, *Why wouldn't people want to do what companies do: sit down and plan where they want to go in life and how they want their lives to be?*

Simultaneously, I was discovering my passion for helping others be successful, both in the workplace and in their own personal development. My opportunities to work with women were much more prevalent after I left the mostly male manufacturing company. I wanted to offer the strategic planning process to women in the form of a workshop. I called it "Personal Strategic Planning," and I submitted my application to run the workshop at *The Women in Management Conference*, run by the University of Southern Maine. Although I had never done anything like this before, I was accepted!

This should have been great news. It was what I had been hoping for! Yet, despite being past my Leap threshold, the ever-present voices of my Threshold Guardians kept telling me, *You can't do it alone. You don't have the credibility. Who do you think you are?* It was difficult to ignore the voices, but I did my best and plunged on.

There were fifteen people in my workshop, fourteen women and one man. They loved the workshop. I loved it. This was great! This was what I wanted to do!

By the end of our day together, they had accomplished what I hoped they would. They had come up with goals for themselves in response to my visioning question, *Given ideal circumstances, what will* my life *look like and be like in three years?*

Even better, six of the women wanted to continue working with me in a small group, meeting monthly. This was my first foray into group coaching, although I didn't know that's what it was called at the time. And from that first workshop grew Ruby Slippers, LLC—a business I started to help women develop a vision for their lives.

There is one major difference between the approach to the *personal* strategic planning process and the *business* planning process. In my personal strategic planning process, women strive to use their intuition rather than their left (logical) brains to answer the visioning question. Unlike what the businesses do, it isn't a process of "figuring it out"—seeing where one fits into predetermined categories—or writing down what you think you "should" do. Instead, it is looking at what emerges from your subconscious and seeing what feels right as your next steps. It is a plan developed organically, from within.

It's what your innermost self wants for you, not what others want for you.

I'd like you to go ahead and try the personal planning process out for yourself. This is the activity that I referred to at the beginning of the chapter that can help you figure out which way to go on your Journey. It helps you find your direction or focus while on the Road.

Task Four: Personal Strategic Planning

For this Task, you're going to be answering one question:

> Given ideal circumstances, what will my life look like
> and be like in three years?

On sticky notes, you'll write your responses. (Yes, that's plural. There will be many.)

Why are you writing on sticky notes by hand? Why not just go to the computer? Wouldn't that be easier? Remember, I just told you this is an organic process originating from within. Your hand-writing of these ideas on paper is the most direct means for you to connect with what's emerging from your psyche. Computer screens and typing don't work as well as the tactile act of putting pen to paper.

I will explain the process further in a moment, but first, read through the following tips for writing your sticky notes.

Tips For Success With Writing Your Sticky Notes

- Use one sticky note for each response to the question. If the word *and* shows up, you may be writing two responses on one sticky. Give each response its own note.

- Write down *all* your responses. Honor everything that comes up by writing it down. There's no limit. Nothing is unreasonable. Nothing is asking for too much. Don't worry about conflicting desires or contradictions.

- If a sticky says something like *My son wins the Nobel Prize*, it's not *your* dream. It's a dream for someone else's life, not your life. These notes can only be about *you*.

- Write in the present tense, as if it's happening now. *I send my essay to a magazine editor. I own a car that works.*

- Be specific. The universe needs to understand what you want. It's like ordering at a restaurant. Instead of writing *a beautiful home* on your sticky, write *a Cape Cod-style home with three dormers.*

- Every sticky note is "right." No dream is too shallow, too selfish or too vain. Write down everything. No self-censorship. It's important to honor your wise inner voice.

Don't worry about memorizing these tips. You can always refer back to them when you're writing your sticky notes.

Now let's get started with the activity.

- **Get yourself out of a left-brained way of operating.** Doing something fun and playful always helps in that regard. (I often have women paint or write with their nondominant hand, tear out pictures from magazines that grab them, or play games they played as children—just to shake them out of their default response, which begins, "I should...") You can run, meditate, walk in nature—anything to get you out of your normal frame of reference. That's why companies go on retreats to do strategic planning. It's easier to see your life more objectively when you're not in the middle of the mundane. You're eager to see a new or different perspective. (I also suggest lighting a candle, getting some tea or other act that creates a sacred space in which to consult your intuition. Do what feels right to you.)

- **Get a blank sheet of paper.** It can be letter-size, although bigger is better. If your paper is letter-sized, you might need several sheets. Give yourself enough room for all your ideas. This blank page represents your future. You're going to add the things you want for your life over the next three years.

- **Get a pad or two of sticky notes and a pen.**

- **Help yourself stay focused.** At the top of the sheet of paper, write:

Given ideal circumstances, what will my life look like and be like in _____ (three years from now)?

- ° Why "ideal" circumstances? Because we don't want to rouse the Threshold Guardians—any nay-saying inner voices or your negative inner critic. If the critic gets into your answers, you'll limit your possibilities right from the start. You'll want to write something like, *I'm exercising every day.* And the critic will shut you up with, *Yeah, right. I've heard you say that before.*

- ° When you hear the Threshold Guardians butting in, please thank them. Their intent, perhaps, is to help you. *Watch out for the stove! You might get burned!* is a useful warning. But right now, you need to hear your own voice, not that of the critic. For this exercise, listen to what comes up inside you without limiting yourself.

- **Envision your future.** Don't start writing yet. In your mind, go to that place where you want to be three years from now. Close your eyes if you like and let your inner senses work. Maybe you'll see pictures. Maybe you'll hear words. What's happening around you? What are you doing? Who are you with? What are you wearing? How do you feel? Watch this movie of your life in three years play out in your mind's eye. Remember, these are *ideal circumstances.* This is your life as you want it to be.

- **Start writing.** Just as the movie of your life three years from now is getting really good, it's time to reach for your sticky notes. Write each of your answers to the question on its own sticky note as quickly as they float up from that wise inner part of you.

- **Keep writing.** As you finish each note, stick it to the blank page that represents your future. If you need more room, use another blank sheet or a larger piece of paper. You'll know you are finished when the ideas start coming more slowly. Stop when you feel you're really straining for ideas.

- **Give yourself a little break.** Go do something else until you feel refreshed.

- **Examine and organize your sticky notes.** Once you're feeling reenergized, it's time to look at the sticky notes scattered all over the blank page of your future. Very shortly, as you read your sticky notes, you'll recognize patterns, categories and common threads. Maybe several sticky notes are about your home or your finances or your family. Start moving sticky notes into groups that relate to each other. There's no prescribed number of groups and no prescribed number of sticky notes in each group. When you've made your groups, use some more sticky notes to title your groups. Some people make neat rows, and others make clusters. Organize the notes in the way that works for you. It's your life. You can do with it what you want. At the end, you'll have something like the example on the following page.

Look at the groups of notes you've made. Do some have many more sticky notes than other categories? The number of notes in a category may reveal certain areas of your life that you most want to change. Sometimes that's a surprise.

Sticky notes may seem to contradict each other at times. For one woman I worked with, one sticky note said, *I have my craft room set up for my weaving,* while another said, *I have my spare room set up for writing.* She worried that she'd have to give up one of her loves because both called for a lot of space and time. Still, she wanted both. Later, she decided that for spring and summer, she would maintain the room for weaving. For fall and winter, she would put the weaving equipment in storage and use the room for writing. The plan gave her enough time and space for both. Contradictory responses don't always mean you must choose one response. Often, they lead you away from false choices toward a life that holds more of what you want.

Given ideal circumstances, what will my life look like/be like in _____ ?

My Finances	About Me	My Writing
I save $500 over the next 6 months	I pay for a good haircut	I send my article to magazines
I pay off one of my credit cards	I do something nice for myself every month	I write every morning for an hour
I talk to HR about increasing my 401K	I go out with my friends regularly	I have published an article
I start a vacation fund	I start saying "no"	I have started my mystery novel

For now, just observe what ended up on your sticky notes, thinking over what you've discovered while you take another break. You can even sleep on it.

In the meantime, you may think of more sticky-note ideas, groupings and connections. Don't hesitate to add or rearrange your notes. Review your notes with these questions in mind:

- Do I want to add categories, remix them or carve out some into subgroups?
- Do I want to add any sticky notes?
- Do I want to reword any sticky notes to make them clearer?
- Are there sticky notes that are not really about me? (*My son has a good job* is not about you. But don't throw it out. You can often transform this desire into an action you can see yourself doing, *I help my son find a career counselor.*)
- Are all my sticky notes about what I want rather than what I think I *should* want?

When you have adjusted your sticky notes and categories to your satisfaction, look over all your category titles and ask yourself this question:

> If I could only focus on one area over the next three years, which would it be?

Whatever your first answer to this question is, remember it, but don't be too quick to accept it. Sometimes, the obvious first priority is something you can't summon the energy to work on until other matters are off your plate, or perhaps it's too scary for you to do right now. Is your first priority only first because you think it *should* be? Consider what would be the most fun or what would give you the most "juice." (Or, as Joseph Campbell said, what's your bliss?) Maybe you'd like to go with that instead. As you ponder the question, give room to what you feel as well as to what you think.

When you've chosen your first priority, mark that category title #1. Now, put #2 on your second choice and #3 on your third choice. Then stop.

What about the rest of the categories?

Put the rest of your categories aside. You already have a very busy life. This process won't work if you reenter your life after your personal strategic planning retreat with too many new things to do.

Therefore, your plan for the next three years is to focus on three areas. You can always add others as you complete the first three. But for now, focus your precious energy on these three specific destinations in your life. Write them down:

Category 1 _____

Category 2 _____

Category 3 _____

Now you're probably feeling great. Maybe you're even thinking, *I'm done!* You're not. But you *are* halfway there. If you don't take the time to do the next step, then you're missing a critical part of the process and your amazing vision for the future might end up tucked away on a shelf as you find yourself stuck in your old routines.

To prevent yourself from falling into your same old ruts, you need to come up with a way of nurturing your vision that will ensure you don't forget the work you just did. We don't want the pull of gravity to bring you back to where you were. You need to develop some written steps to take you forward. Here's how you do it.

Look at your three categories. Choose one or two of the sticky notes from each category to be your main goals in those areas. It will look like this (using our earlier example):

Category 1: Finances
   Goal 1—I pay off one of my credit cards.
   Goal 2—I start a vacation fund.

Category 2: About Me
   Goal 1—I do something nice for myself every month.
   Goal 2—I start saying "no."

Category 3: My Writing
   Goal 1—I write every morning for an hour.
   Goal 2—I have started my mystery novel.

Once you've chosen your goals, the next step is to decide on the actions or steps needed to make those goals happen. Keep reading for some useful hints and ways to record these steps.

Before you zoom off to write your action steps, beware that people tend to be overly ambitious with this part. So, before you continue, let me share an important tip. *Be realistic with your timeline for completing your action steps.* (Exhibits A and B illustrate what I mean.)

Let's consider, for example, "Category 3: My Writing, Goal 2—I have started my mystery novel." Exhibit A shows what not to do.

Exhibit A

Actions I Need to Take to Accomplish Goal 2— I have started my mystery novel

What I'm Going to Do:	I'll start this step by:	I'll finish this step by:	How I'll reward myself:
Write Chapter 1	May 1	May 15	
Write Chapter 2	May 16	May 31	
Complete Novel	June 1	June 30	

What I'm Going to Do:	I'll start this step by:	I'll finish this step by:	How I'll reward myself:
Send to publisher	July 1		Champagne brunch with friends

Do you see the problem? The schedule is far too aggressive! Are there people who complete a novel in two months? Maybe! But it's probably not realistic for most people.

Remember, you started this process with a full plate. You've identified or added three areas in your life on which to focus. You need to start with small steps or you won't be able to fit it all in. Things will slip, you'll get discouraged, and you'll quit.

Now, look at Exhibit B. It's the same example but with smaller, more realistic, action steps. The disclaimer: if you want to go gang-busters on whatever your goal is and you feel like you have the ability to do it, that's fine! Trust yourself! This will all materialize differently for each person.

Exhibit B

Actions I Need to Take to Accomplish Goal 2— I have started my mystery novel

What I'm Going to Do:	I'll start this step by:	I'll finish this step by:	How I'll reward myself:
Decide on schedule and process for writing	May 1	May 15	Walk with dogs

What I'm Going to Do:	I'll start this step by:	I'll finish this step by:	How I'll reward myself:
Begin Chapter 1 to test how I'll write (when, where, etc.)	May 16	May 20	No writing on weekends
Adjust schedule and process accordingly, after test	May 23	May 24	
Continue writing 1st Chapter	May 25	July 31	Brunch with friends

Now it's your turn! You can either create your own document to capture these commitments or download a template for this chart, as well as other related resources, at susannaliller.com/youareaheroine.

Okay… So maybe you don't like working linearly. That's alright! Mind mapping is another way to complete this task (once you have your sticky notes finished). A mind map is a visual diagram used to represent your ideas.

Start with a circle in the center. If you're mind mapping this task, the center circle is one of your three main sticky-note categories. Write in the category title. Next, draw lines coming out of your category circle—like spokes on a wheel. These are for the goals you chose for each of your categories. Write them in. Finally, draw lines coming out from each goal. These are for your action steps, dates and rewards.

On the following page is one way to mind map your plan. Mind maps are always unique. Google them to see other examples. Create your Category-Goal-Action Steps mind map however it works for you.

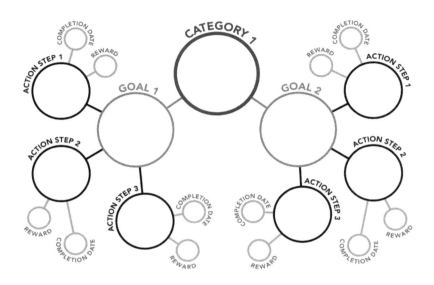

Have you started working on your action steps and already determined that you've been overzealous, cramming too much into your first week or first month? It's OK. Just adjust your steps. Do one thing a week… or month, if that's better. The point is to do *something* to move in the direction you want to go.

At the same time, pay attention! Be on the lookout for opportunities, for doors opening, and for signs that could point the way or even fulfill your goals. The cues could be subtle.

Say that one of your goals is to take more time for yourself. When your friend spontaneously invites you to go on a vacation, don't miss the opportunity to fulfill your goal, even if it's not how you planned to do it. It may not be happenstance. Maybe this is your focused intention making things happen for you sooner than you thought.

One Last Thing along Those Same Lines

There is a phenomenon I've noticed during my twenty-five years of using this approach with people. When someone becomes clear on what they want to focus on, when they hold the image of it in their consciousness, when they take some steps toward making it happen, they often draw to them experiences that are inexplicable synchronicities. These could be interpreted either as chance or as a direct response to their intention.

What's going on here?

If you're of the "chance" frame of mind, then you can stop right here and just be grateful for your good fortune. But how do you explain it if, like me, you feel there's more at work here—that it is a response to your intention?

You have a power source within you. It's the combined power of your thoughts and feelings. I call it the "power of intention."

When you activate it in a positive way, you can draw to you what you want.

Does it work that way all the time? No.

Do I understand how it works? No.

But it has worked for me and for many others. I know it can work for you.

Your intentions are on the sticky notes. You allowed them to float up into your consciousness, and you honored them by writing them down. You organized them and committed to putting your energy into changing three areas of your life. You have set something in motion, so expect to see a result.

Can you block it? Yes. Negative thinking is one of the best ways to block it. Focusing on what you *don't* want will block it. But would you have taken the time to go through this process if you didn't believe at least a little bit that something could come of it?

All you need is a little bit of faith that your thoughts, feelings and intentions have power. Just a little bit of faith will bring results.

And one more thought… Just like Doing a Circle, don't try to figure out how your vision will turn up or materialize. Usually it comes by a circuitous route that you couldn't have predicted. Just let go and let the universe work.

Full Disclosure: There have been times when people I've worked with don't nurture their visions at all. They write their sticky notes, put them in groups on their white boards, come up with their top three categories, and then put them away. And that's it. They don't do anything more, and then they'll tell me, "A year later, I found my stickies, looked at them, and was amazed that most of them had happened!"

How to explain this? Maybe your subconscious somehow shifts into gear when you get intentional, and then it goes on autopilot. I don't know, but this has happened more than once, so I feel compelled to let you know.

Still, I recommend that you at least put your board somewhere visible and look at the sticky notes every now and then (hanging on the inside of a closet door is a commonly used spot). The stickies represent your vision for your life three years from now. That's important! Seeing them refreshes that vision, giving it energy and keeping it in the forefront of your consciousness.

You've done the work. You took the time. Good for you. Now, you can let go of micromanaging it. Work on your action steps. Attend to the day-to-day. But pay attention and see what comes your way. It might surprise you. Your dreams might just show up.

Chapter 9

The Guardian of Your Fears

The Dragon

All of these dragon killings and threshold crossings have to do with getting past being stuck.

— Joseph Campbell, *The Power Of Myth*

Secrets, when exposed to the light of day, are completely disempowered. They're monsters in your closet. When you turn the light on it, it was a dress after all. It was a shadow.

— Pamela McCreary, *Real-Life Heroine*

Any Heroine who has previously taken a Leap or risked starting another adventure knows that at some point there will be a reckoning—something she needs to learn about herself and her life. That reckoning is when we meet up with The Dragon.

The Dragon is all about fears—fears that come to the surface when you Leap, fears that perhaps began in childhood and shaped the beliefs you have about yourself and the world. The Journey often brings these fears forward where you must face them and heal them. These deep fears that can keep us from the treasure of becoming our own authentic self are our Dragons.

Pamela, who left the Mormon Church and her husband during her Journey, shares with us about her personal Dragon:

> The fear for me, I think, was what [will] people think if they [know] what happened? If they really know me, they won't like me. I think that for a lot of us, there is a deep little Dragon who rears its ugly head, breathes fire, scorches us and then runs away again. All of us probably have had our eyebrows singed a time or two from that Dragon. That is why it was so cathartic to put my book out there. Someone reads this book and they know me. They know me and they can choose to like me or not. But there was power for me in telling my truth. I needed to do it to conquer my Dragon.

Former U.S. team cyclist Maureen also tells us about her fears (her Dragons) and how she took charge of them:

> I was twelve years into my diagnosis of MS when I began to compete in triathlons. I kept practicing my philosophy of focusing on what I *could* do. It expanded my life. It felt magical being able to be out there and competitive, but I still had these huge fears of racing my bicycle. When all these fears came bombarding me, I focused on what I had learned in my journey—to not run from the fears but to listen to them and learn how to be with them. I mean there is all the stuff like:
> What if you can't do it?
> What if you hurt yourself?
> What if you hurt somebody else?
> What if you can't be competitive?
> Before the diagnosis, I had risen to the highest category on the national team. I was a national champion. I wasn't going to come back and make a fool of myself.
> At another time, those thoughts would have been

enough to close the door, but I had learned to say to those fears, "Come here, let's sit," and then start knocking them off one by one. FEAR can be an acronym for "Feeling Emotion and Running." The emotions that are associated with your fears are painful. But we can learn to breathe with the fears, be with them, befriend them, and let them teach us.

I started training by joining small groups and riding to see how that felt. I knew when a big challenge came to me that if I entertained the fears it would be all over. But I also knew to listen to myself... that the fear was there, but there was also the excitement. When they are both there, then I know it's mine to do. I went for it.

When Lisa was able to let go of teaching music, her Dragon taught (and continues to teach) her to be willing to disappoint:

One Dragon I have to keep working on is disengaging from approval and being willing to disappoint other people. It keeps coming up for me. It's something I keep working on. I think it's big for a lot of women, because we put ourselves out there as caregivers and people are dependent on us. I placed a lot of responsibility on myself to fulfill what I perceived to be my duties and obligations with my family, my clients and my former business partners.

Being coached and coaching others has helped me differentiate between what I'm projecting onto other people as their expectations of me, versus what's real. It's a tough one for me. I really want everyone to be happy. And it can't be that way.

What about You?

Does the same negative stuff keep happening to you? Do you know there's something that you need to address, but you're unwilling to go there? Do you feel like you're stuck?

If you answered "yes" to any of these questions, then maybe there's a Dragon on your path.

We all have this "shadow" stuff inside us. We tend to feel shame and embarrassment about it. *I can't let anyone know about* _____. Yet the fact is, we *all* have something similarly shadowy. It goes along with being human. It is definitely part of the Journey!

You go on the Journey to meet the challenges that birth you—evolve you—into a more heroic self. This is how women become Heroines. We don't shirk going into the abyss, into the dark (inner Journey) to confront what needs confronting.

This part of the Journey is not for the faint of heart. It can be tempting to skip. You'll think you've gotten through, done the work, but—surprise! You've only been fooling yourself. With time, you'll find yourself saying, *I never did address my pattern of* _____ (whatever your particular challenge may be). *Maybe that's why it keeps reappearing to stop me or keep me stuck.*

So, you dig. And, if you're really vigilant and honest with your digging, then a talon will appear, followed by a scaly tail, a leg or two, a pearly wing, and then there she is—the Dragon you're confronting on this particular Heroine's Journey cycle. Here's the thing you may not know about your Dragon: she's actually really glad to see you. She's been wondering what's taken you so long. She's exclaiming, *I didn't even think you cared about me!*

She's been faithfully guarding something that you haven't wanted to address, even if you haven't consciously known that that something existed. She's guarding what she sees as your "treasure." She's done it to protect you. And now, here you two are, face-to-face. You need to get her to release your treasure—some vital part of yourself that needs to be brought into the light. Only then will you have more freedom to be yourself. What is your Dragon guarding?

You thought you'd be afraid of her, but you realize there's no reason to be. She's beautiful. Of course she is, because she's part of you. Take her in fully... the magnificence of her body, her wings, her expressive eyes filled with love—all for you. And the meaning of *self-love* becomes clearer as we learn to love *all* parts of ourselves, even the parts we might not be proud of.

Face it, and then let it go. You will be glad you did.

Remember my story of leaving the manufacturing company with Brenda (the Leap) and the subsequent ups and downs that occurred on the Road of Adventure? We were together, having great success, and then to my distress, she left me. I moved forward and did it myself, proving that I can do it alone. My Dragon for that Heroine's Journey was undoubtedly my deep-seated fear that I can't do big things alone.

When I began examining my Dragon (my fear), I realized I knew exactly how she had entered my life. Growing up, I had very protective parents and a beloved grandmother who lived with us (yes, the same grandmother who jumped from the train). The three of them watched over me very carefully. I didn't do much alone as a child. I couldn't even cross the street by myself to go to my elementary school. It was never their intent that, from their avid care, I would derive a fear of independence. Yet that is exactly what happened. As children we often misinterpret the messages we receive from those around us. We ingest them as deep beliefs and act accordingly, often well into our adult lives. These false beliefs live within us and steer our actions.

From my family's diligent care, I took to heart that I wasn't safe or couldn't manage alone and needed to depend upon others. My experience with Brenda put this issue front and center for me. The fear after she left was very real. It was visceral. But because I had to move through it to keep my business going,

I had to look fear in the eye and address it head on. What was this fear about?

I realized that this had been my pattern. I remembered times in the past when I had clung to others for a false sense of safety, because I believed I wasn't OK doing it alone or even being alone. And until the Brenda experience, it was all unconscious.

How many of those early messages do we misinterpret yet still have within us as lurking Dragons? If you learn to look for them, you'll see that they come up in order for you to heal them. Bravery is required if you're going to do the inner work that brings Dragons to the surface, the work that every Heroine needs to do on her Journey.

Meet your Dragons, get to know them, and heal whatever it was that created them. This takes courage. Some people would rather go into physical battle than explore what's going on within their own psyche, but this is the work that will ensure our actions are the right ones for us. Yes, you can always choose to leave your Dragons alone in the dark, but the freedom you achieve by releasing them is one of the big gifts of the Heroine's Journey.

There's a delightful children's book called *There's No Such Thing as a Dragon* by Jack Kent.[9] In the story, young Billy Bixbee wakes up one morning to a small adorable dragon sitting at the foot of his bed. He runs downstairs to tell his mother, who insists, "There's no such thing as a dragon!"

Billy believes her (of course he does—she's his mother) and continues about his day ignoring this dragon, as does his mom. The dragon then proceeds to grow bigger and bigger and bigger. It gets larger than the house, and when the bread truck goes by, it runs after it, carrying the house on its back—with Mom and Billy inside screaming for help. It's at this point that Dad shows up.

"How did this happen?" Mr. Bixbee asked.

"It was the dragon," said Billy.

"There's no such thing—" Mother started to say.

"There *is* a dragon!" Billy insisted. "A very *big* dragon!" And Billy patted the dragon on the head.

Thank you, Billy! And kudos to all of you who can look into your shadowy self and see that, yes, there is a Dragon… and then begin to deal with it.

In the story, as soon as Billy acknowledges the dragon, the dragon begins to shrink and goes back to being as small as he was in the beginning.

"I don't mind dragons *this* size," said Mother. "Why did it have to grow so *big*?"

"I'm not sure," said Billy, "but I think it just wanted to be noticed."

It's important to notice, make peace with and, ultimately, love our Dragons.

Chapter 10

There's No Place Like Home

The Return Threshold

The effect of the successful adventure of the hero is the unlocking and release again of the flow of life into the body of the world.

— Joseph Campbell, *The Hero with a Thousand Faces*

I think it's so compelling that your first reaction was, "No, not me, I'm not a heroine. Their journey is so much more difficult (or impressive or whatever)." And isn't it so true that we all feel that way? But then somebody gives us another perspective and says, "Are you kidding me? Look at what you've accomplished!"

— Pamela McCreary, *Real-Life Heroine*

Now we're at the end. Well, nearly the end. There's still a Return Threshold to cross. We are done with this particular Journey, and we're headed back to the village whence we began. Yes, perhaps it's the same Ordinary Life that we were experiencing before we went on this Heroine's Journey, but we've changed. We return, altered in some way. We collect our Gifts Received and review what this Journey has given us. And because we've confronted or befriended our Dragons, we've recovered and integrated a bit more of ourselves into what is now a more authentic self.

We are freer to be our true selves with every trip we take around the Journey milestones. Maybe we are less intent on pleasing or controlling others, or we're not as other-focused as we were before. Maybe we're braver or more compassionate.

Every Journey is unique to the traveler. It will release the Gifts that each individual needs. With each Journey, we become more comfortable in our own skin and appreciate, to a greater degree, who we are. Campbell called this "the Freedom to Live"—the exhilarating freedom we feel when we can be ourselves.

In addition to the Freedom to Live, I have found that there are three central gifts that most Heroines receive from their Journey— the boons that the Journey leads you to discover. These three gifts are **Identity**, **Direction** and **Power**. They are powerful keys that you can use to unlock the doors within you, ultimately yielding a fulfilled life.

Gift One: Identity

On the Journey, you become clearer about who you are. You encounter challenges, situations or people who reveal to you something about yourself. As the Heroine, you discover a repeated pattern of experience that leads you to realize you are exhibiting an old survival behavior that you don't need anymore. You decide to discard it and voilà—you've uncovered a bit more of the "real" Heroine within.

You learn how to remove your armor, disguises and defenses... all the things you've donned or learned to exist safely in this world. You come to see that this uncovering or authenticating process is what it means to be self-aware. It's what you, the Heroine, do. You practice self-reflection. You work to discover your own true traits, distinct from what's been added on or unconsciously adopted from others.

The Heroine's Journey helps you understand that you are strong and powerful... You are a Heroine. You might not be using your Heroineism at the moment, but it is your potential, what you can grow into.

How can you claim an identity unless you have an awareness of it? By becoming aware of what constitutes your Heroineism, I hope that you can look at what you've already done and see that you've earned the title of "Heroine."

Consider women's suffrage. Before they were given the right to vote, until their awareness was raised, women didn't even think of themselves as potential voters. They didn't see it in their universe of possibilities. Then, as Susan B. Anthony and others began to speak and write that it was the right of women to vote, more and more women got on board. It was a huge paradigm shift.

Seeing yourself as a Heroine is a paradigm shift too. Men are heroes. We think heroism is about big masculine events like rescuing people from a fire or winning a battle. We are accustomed to a male view of courage and bravery. Heroineism is about having the courage to expand from within. Yes, it may involve physical feats, but it is more about doing what broadens your view of yourself and stretching your inner limits.

If I could make a movie of your life and show you what you've been through, show you the decisions you did or didn't make, it would exemplify the milestones of the Journey, as lived by a Heroine.

Recognize who you are. You are the movie star playing *you, the Heroine*, in real life and in real-time.

Gift Two: Direction

The Heroine's Journey can serve as your compass in a seemingly directionless world. Life is about taking that Journey, as many times as you need to. The Journey is defined by the major milestones. The first storytellers were recounting what we still hear today: leave your comfort zones!

When you do leave in response to a Call, the milestones ahead of you are guaranteed. People will try to dissuade and help you. You will feel like you're tossing and turning in a soupy mess of confusion. You will find yourself confronted with situations that challenge your beliefs about yourself and about the world. And eventually, you'll come out of it with new insights, a shift in your reality, or a growth in awareness. (And what if you don't get the full a-ha moment this time around? Rest assured, there will be another Call to lead you over the Threshold again.)

There are pivotal points on the Journey. If you've Crossed the Threshold and you're on the Road, there will be times when you have to make a decision about which way to go. There are so many *Now what? Now where to?* parts of our life. Often a woman I'm coaching will tell me she doesn't know where she wants to go. She just knows she doesn't want to be where she is. This is where knowing how to access your intuition is useful.

The Personal Strategic Planning task in chapter 8 is a tool to help you find your way, a divining rod of sorts, especially if you've never been sure who to listen to when it comes to finding your direction. Have you always followed a parent's or partner's advice? Are you guided by the prevailing trends? Maybe you tend to defer to the advice of whoever is offering it?

By taking the Heroine's Journey and doing your work, you instead learn to hear your inner Heroine's voice, letting that be your guiding compass.

Gift Three: Power

There are two aspects to the power that you gain through taking the Heroine's Journey: internal and external.

Internal power comes from uncovering your authentic self. When you become more responsible for your own decisions, and when those decisions come from within rather than from outside sources, then you shed the old behaviors and strategies that you learned (mostly unconsciously) in order to fit in, get ahead or stay safe. Instead of living in response to what you think others want, which gives away your power, you start living by your own moral compass, your truths. Only then do you become yourself, operating out of your own desires, beliefs and feelings rather than in reaction to others. You believe in you! This is power. Being authentic is powerful. As a Heroine, you learn to connect to your inner voice and internally grow your own power source.

The external aspect of power refers to a spiritual power, however you refer to it: God, higher power, spirit, energy, the universe or "guiding hands," as Campbell called it. Whatever you name this source, finding your external power is about acknowledging that you have unseen help.

If this is something you believe in and want to do, you can learn to connect to this power source and ask it for guidance and help in co-creating. This is another level of power, and it requires commitment, practice and discipline to access it. It requires intentionality to make the connection happen. (Calling it an "external power" can be misleading since many find this divine, spiritual spark within themselves. Regardless, if you feel it is within or believe spirit exists outside of yourself, it is still a power that is available to all Heroines.)

The more times you take the Heroine's Journey, the more you access these three gifts:

- **Identity** (know yourself)
- **Direction** (know your way... or how to find it)
- **Power** (know your authentic truth, internal and external)

In addition to the three primary Gifts Received, every Heroine receives individualized gifts. Our three Heroines share with us what they learned and what gifts they received. They tell us how the Journey out of their comfort zones, leaping into the void of the unknown, gave them more freedom to be themselves.

The boon, or gift, of Pamela's Journey was learning the power of telling her truth.

> I didn't start out to write a book. I began journaling to make sense of my life. I was twice divorced and another relationship had ended, badly. I was sick of making the same mistake and needed clarity. I have come to learn there is much value in writing for anyone who wants to look at their life.
>
> Writing my book was cathartic, and I didn't hold anything back. I don't exactly paint myself in the most flattering light at times, but I am committed to telling the truth. There is power in truth-telling. Secrets steal your authenticity.
>
> I think each of us is longing for and searching for our true self, the one who is authentic, that speaks to the core of who we really are.
>
> Somebody reads my book and they know me. They know *me* and they can choose to like me or not. But there was power for me in telling my truth. It was the gift that came from this journey.

Maureen found the gift of compassion—compassion for herself—on her Journey.

> So how do I expand the possible? These are some of the nuggets of how I continue to challenge my assumptions of what I think I can and can't do.
>
> I didn't know what I could do. But what I knew was that I wouldn't know until I tried, until I went for it, and then I would know. That's where the answers were, not in the fears.
>
> I certainly find my limits. And compassion is vital. If you go outside of your comfort zone, there lie the dragons: the self-doubts, the concerns and all that

stuff. If you can't inspire yourself with self-compassion, then it's going to be a miserable journey. It's going to be a painful journey if we're beating ourselves up. Compassion is vital.

Lisa brought back the gift of how to find her inner voice.

We go through these transitions (as represented by the Heroine's Journey) and they take us into a different territory, into a deeper part of ourselves. Perhaps we grow into what are very different versions of ourselves. It will involve letting go of some old stories that have been outgrown. But we also have to embrace those old selves as part of the whole.

I think that in terms of letting go and reconciling big identity changes, it's been important for me to acknowledge that where I came from is also part of me. And those parts enabled me to make that move. It's about acknowledging and being curious about everything you are and have ever been and could be.

Going through transition is like training a muscle. We have this mental resistance to crossing before we do it, because we are dreading the process of letting go, the fear, this uncertain place we are going into. But the more we practice taking small steps into that unknown and taking small steps out of our comfort zone, the stronger we get.

We have to find that comfort-zone edge all the time. It's always moving. Hopefully, as we gain experience and we learn more, the edge expands. Going toward it and stepping across it continuously is what brings that aliveness and joy to life.

I've learned there is a value in not doing anything for certain periods of time. It's about us having the ability to be still, make the space, create the silence, to listen to that. That's what I mean by stillness: to actually be able to hear your inner voice. We can choose thoughts that support what we are longing to be, or we can choose to believe the ones that hold us back.

What about You?

Are you able to recount the gifts you gained on your past Journeys, even the most difficult ones?

Have you given yourself the compassion you deserve when you've looked back at the challenges (Dragons) you've faced?

Did some, or all, of the Journeys help you recover a little more of your authentic self?

Have you realized that we're all going through this same Journey and you're not alone?

What treasure did you bring back from your Journey? In Greek mythology, Jason and his Argonauts brought back the Golden Fleece. In *The Wizard of Oz,* Dorothy learned how much she loved her Aunt Em and Uncle Henry and her home. You're not a storybook Heroine, so your gifts probably aren't that specific or tangible, but I'll bet that they're much more valuable.

And remember, when you share these gifts with others, they become a boon for society. So, when you cross the Return Threshold and travel back into "civilization," you can bring these gifts to others—the most important being the gift of *you* as an authentic, focused and empowered woman.

It's vital to remember and reflect on all the gifts we receive from each Heroine's Journey. They remind us why we Journey.

As many rewards as they bring, Journeys are still difficult. If they were easy, then I'd be writing about the Heroine's Vacation, which wouldn't be much of a book because who really changes on their vacation? But Journeys *do* change us.

Writing this book has certainly changed me. And as I cross

the Return Threshold with the gifts I've received along the way, I am reminded that taking a Journey is how we expand our capacity to be who we are in this lifetime. We do what we initially think we can't do.

The Heroine's Journey calls us to step out over that chasm and Leap. That Call may seem crazy to us at the time, but if we answer it, the subsequent Journey will undeniably lead us to a more brilliant life than we ever thought possible.

Chapter 11

Hearing Our Collective Call:
Women, Unite!

Bill Moyers: ...we're not on our journey to save the world but to save ourselves.
Joseph Campbell: But in doing that you save the world. The influence of a vital person vitalizes.

— Joseph Campbell, *The Power Of Myth*

Feminine wounds are almost always cured by being still. A man, or the masculine side of a woman, generally has to take an outwardly heroic stance with his problems. Our mythology is full of the heroic man who mounts his white horse and goes galloping off to do the heroic deed, which is his way of addressing the wrongs of life... But woman's genius is quite the reverse.

— Robert A. Johnson,
The Fisher King & The Handless Maiden

It's time to come down from the mountaintop, from the wider perspective this book offers, and go back to living your Journey, wherever you are on the road. Thank you for taking the time to look at the Journey landscape with me... the sandpits, the sparkling streams, the lairs of the wild beasts, the hilltops and valleys, the dark parts in the dense forest that look the most frightening but reveal the greatest insights.

Review your life and see how courageous you've been. You've taken Leaps in response to the Calls of the Journey—the Journey to be your own true self. No matter how little or big, how recent or long past, let those Leaps stand out for you like beacons. They are badges of your achievements as a woman of courage and as a woman who listens to and respects her own inner voice.

Your Leaps are perceptible challenges that you have overcome, but may I remind you that you have also faced a significant subliminal challenge throughout your Journey? It is something that you may have felt but did not see: the challenge to focus on yourself. To travel your Journey well, you must, at least momentarily, turn your attention away from the world and toward yourself. The difficulty is that doing this opposes the cultural expectation that women should care for everyone else. Focusing on yourself may not come naturally for you, but it is imperative to do so in order to find your way on your Journeys. And equally important is to do it with compassion (as Maureen reminded us in chapter 10).

I think back to some of my most powerful Heroine's Journeys: leaving my first marriage, starting my own consulting company, beginning a new marriage, and starting Ruby Slippers, LLC. (And of course, raising my children... any mother can attest to that monumental Journey!) When I stepped into the unknown of each of these adventures, they were full of the risks, trials and tests every Journey holds. Some challenges of the Journeys were physical, while others were mental or emotional. Sometimes, I could see what I was facing, and other times I could only feel it. But I made it through it all. And now I can look back and reaffirm that each Journey was just the right thing for me to do. Each one played such a big part in shaping me into the strong and (mostly) sure woman I am today. (Maybe after a few more Journeys I will be able to remove the "mostly" from that sentence!)

Because I dared to venture outside my comfort zone, my life is much richer and more multidimensional. The thirty-five-year-old version of me who, with such trepidation, told her husband that she wanted a divorce, seems like someone from a different life. But she is me and, looking back, I love her dearly and have such compassion for her. I find that assessing our past Journeys helps us recall and appreciate the gifts we've received. And maybe equally important, it brings us more compassion for ourselves.

We'll need that compassion for the selves we are today, so that we don't we forget what we've already done as we stand with one foot hesitating over a new threshold.

Are you doubting that you can do what your current Call is asking you to do? Please! Remember those Leaps you've taken and how they made you into the Heroine you are today. You are brave. You are wise. And your bravery and wisdom grow, one begetting the other, with each Journey you take.

Listen to the inspirational wisdom of our Heroines: Pamela, Maureen and Lisa. Their insights have come from their many Journeys.

Pamela

We need to understand that none of us are victims of our circumstance. We are victims of what we *think of* as our circumstances. *That is the one thing we can change: the way we look at things.* I have learned that no amount of trying can change the past, but I can choose the way the past affects me by altering the way I view it. The less power I give to the past, the more power I have in the present. The more empowered I am, the more strength I have to give to myself and others.

Maureen

It is in the *action* that we discover ourselves. It doesn't have to be a huge action. It can be a small action...

Courage isn't something we are born with. *Courage is earned. It's something we get by acting.* It's like we build our courage muscle and, in doing so, we learn more about ourselves and our authentic and true selves. We also gain an understanding and are able to move with our authentic power.

Lisa

I was agonizing over decisions, thinking, "What do I want to do?" Then finally there was a moment when I knew. It was a quiet moment when I was contemplating the very next step I was going to take. I knew what I needed to do. *I've learned there is actually value in not doing anything for a time.* So that's what I mean by stillness: to actually be able to hear your inner voice.

Pamela, Maureen and Lisa are consciously living the Heroine's Journey and reaping its wisdom. Hear their voices and the echoing message of the Heroine's Journey:

- The one thing we can change is the way we look at things. *We can view our lives from a different perspective, through a much broader lens, that of the Heroine's Journey.*
- Courage is earned. It's something we get by taking action. *We have to answer the Call and make the Leap.*
- There is value in not doing anything and being still for a time. *The answers are within you, if you can just find solitude, get quiet and listen.*

You've heard this wisdom before, maybe from your women friends, your mother, a grandmother or aunt, when you go to them with a problem. This is collective wisdom, gained and shared by women everywhere, Journey after Journey, generation after generation.

And I wonder… I wonder if this collective wisdom is a whole that is equal to more than the sum of its parts. Imagine, if you will, that you're standing in front of the largest, most exquisite tapestry in the world. When you look at it up close—so close that your nose is almost touching it—you can see that the tapestry is made up of hundreds of thousands of tiny threads. But when you step back and view the tapestry from a distance, the individual threads blend together to create a stunning work of art. Collective wisdom is like this tapestry. Every Journey ever taken by any woman is a thread. Each unique thread, by itself, is limited in its value and strength. But woven together with millions of others, the parts become something bigger, something unbreakable and beautiful, something to be passed down through history.

Collective wisdom is a valuable guide for your Journey, helping you find your way. But please don't think of it as an instruction manual with step-by-step directions. There is no correct way to travel your Heroine path. Just like the individual threads in a tapestry, every Call, every Leap and every Journey is unique, from one Journey to the next and from one woman to another. What you have to do to Cross the Threshold differs from what everyone else has to do. For some of you, the Journey leads you to conquer the world of business or politics or social causes, riding in on your own charger and making your mark. For others, it may be the opposite. The Journey may be showing you that you must turn away from the world for a while, become quiet and find your bearings.

No matter where your Journey is leading you, I believe that our individual Journeys all somehow contribute to the larger whole… aiding *all* women. I know that the story of my grandmother's jump from the train has inspired and motivated me since she first told it to me. But I'm also thinking of our deeper connection as women. Perhaps the more we honor our intuition, the more we believe in it and trust, value and respond to it—developing our inner guidance systems as a result—the more we're all lifted up together, our power exponentially increased.

This will lead us to trust more in the genius of our feminine nature so we can discover and heal, in our own unique way, our psychological wounds and ultimately the cultural and ecological wounds of the planet. After all, as our ancient ancestors and indigenous peoples believed (and still believe), we women *are* the planet—we are Mother Earth. If we aren't fed and nourished, everything suffers. The way we treat ourselves and each other is reflected in our care of the planet.

So then, let's consider all of us women as a whole… where are we on the Heroine's Journey?

Are we in the Belly of the Whale?

Are we floundering in the abyss, about to face our collective Dragon?

I see us on a new Threshold. We've probably been hanging out there for a while. I don't think we've been refusing the Call. I think we've been figuring out the Call—what we're collectively hearing—and we're weighing how to respond.

What's been our Ordinary Life? For thousands of years now, we've been the aid and support of our male partners. Many of us truly want to be that support, but we also feel the Call to become more. We've been hearing this Call for a while. The Threshold Guardians have been very active, telling us to stand back! Many of us feel threatened as we step out of our comfort zones. The warnings come from all sides, including within. *Women, you can't have it all. You thought you could, but you can't.* These voices have left us with questions. *What is our role? Do we lean in or do we step back?*

I think we're on the Threshold of creating a new paradigm, a new myth, for women. We aren't solely the tenders of the hearth that we used to be. We aren't only the female replacement of the male in the boardroom. We're both of these and more.

So, what does our new myth look like?

The truth is, I don't know.

We have to develop it together. We have to know our stories and share them with each other. What I do believe is that we will arrive at our new feminine myth in our own unique way, rather than the conventional, more masculine "figuring it out" method. It will come to us through those same inner currents that generate music, poetry, art and literature. It will enter our psyches at a deeper, more subterranean level. Like the wisdom and guidance that comes into our awareness from an unsuspected source, it will be there when we start listening.

Maybe the answers we seek will move in like a freight train. Or perhaps they will tiptoe into our consciousness. The answers might crash down on us as we try to wrestle with our problems, or maybe they'll softly settle in our psyches as we listen to a story.

I have one such story in mind... an old tale from the Brothers Grimm, "The Handless Maiden." It's a Journey story that holds wisdom that's been passed down through generations with every telling. I'll give you a synopsis of it and, as you read, consider its message.

> One day, the Devil comes to make a bargain with a miller. He offers to show the miller a way to improve the laborious task of grinding grain. He says he'll make the mill go faster if, in exchange, he can have what's behind the man's mill. The man agrees to the bargain, thinking that the Devil means a tree standing behind the mill... but horrors, he actually means the miller's daughter! The Devil, after helping the miller, cuts off the daughter's hands and takes them as he leaves.
>
> The daughter has a hard time of it. She relies on her parents' care once her hands are gone. She complains to her mother that she cannot do anything, but her mother tells her she doesn't have to. Depressed and unhappy, she finally breaks down weeping and can't stop.

For solace, she leaves and goes into the woods. (By the way, the woods are always more than what they appear in fairy tales. In this story, they represent the miller's daughter going within to find answers and her own way in the world.) By chance, the path leads her to a king's garden. In true fairytale fashion, she and the king fall in love and marry. The king fashions beautiful silver hands for her and she becomes lauded throughout the kingdom for her hands.

For a while, the maiden-turned-queen is happy, even though she still feels useless and dependent because she lacks real hands. She and the king are blessed with a son, and everything goes well for a time, because she has so many servants to help her. But then it happens again—one day, she starts weeping and can't stop. The king tries to console her, just as her mother did, telling her she doesn't have to do anything, but the tears keep coming.

The queen chooses the same path of healing that she did when she was a maiden… she goes into the forest. She needs time to get in touch with herself, in solitude. She brings her son, and they live there for a while. But how can she exist on her own? Then her Dragon—her deep-seated fear—comes into play, echoing what everyone else has told her: she can't do anything, she must be dependent, she must be happy and let everyone wait on her.

If this is really true, her life has no meaning. Suddenly, the Journey offers up something unexpected: opportunity in the guise of calamity! While playing by a stream, her son falls in. Without hands, she cannot rescue him! She calls for help, but no one can hear her.

In her desperation to save her son, the queen forgets
that her silver hands are useless and plunges them into
the stream, lifting the boy to safety. She has done it!
She can take action and be successful. She has power!
And as an added miracle, her silver hands become real
flesh-and-blood hands. Like every Journey, the queen's
Journey bestows its gifts: transformation and rebirth.

The maiden-queen is thrust onto a Journey of physical hard-
ship as a result of an apparent blunder of her father's. But she finds
that others are taking care of her. Are they mentors? Helpers?
They sound more like Threshold Guardians. *Let me take care of
you. Don't go. Stay safe!*

She leads a life of dependency, first with her parents, then with
the king. Both times, though, it's her tears that lead her to seek
solitude. Our emotions are excellent guides.

The maiden-queen's need for solitude directs her at several
important points on her Journey. First, it leads her to a life with
the king, where she finds love, receives silver hands and has a son.
Then, her need for solitude directs her into the Abyss, where she
comes face-to-face with her Dragon—the fear that she can't do
anything for herself. (You'll remember that I know this Dragon
well.) But she *does* do it herself. She saves her son and, in so doing,
heals herself.

Perhaps you can see yourself in the handless maiden story, but
do you also see that the maiden-queen is like womankind? Yes,
we may have real hands, but in many other ways we have been
limited—by society, by our families, by our own beliefs. We ask
in frustration, *What can we do about this?*

Have we women allowed society to make a "devil's bargain"
for us? How many times have we exchanged some part of our
precious selves to be accommodating to others? Have we been
enticed and silenced with the promise of silver hands—something
that, while beautiful, still renders us useless? Have we been taught

that we can't take care of ourselves—that it's OK to be dependent? And how many tears have we shed after trying (and failing) to conform to the desires of society? Our feelings will always communicate when something needs attention and when something needs to change. Desperation leads us to action. It can unite us to work together to transform our lives.

When we are ready, we need to trust ourselves, both on an individual level and on a collective level. We do know what to do. We can go into "the woods" and find a way to get quiet and connect to our own wisdom. We can start listening to what our own intuition is telling us. We'll hear our Call and understand how to respond. The path will make itself visible again, and we'll emerge strong, with hands and heart ready to do what needs to be done.

We women have access to abundant wisdom: the growing wisdom within ourselves and the collective feminine wisdom around us. We have to believe in ourselves and in each other. Furthermore, we need to believe that there is value not only in having our voices heard but also in sharing our stories and discerning our way... *together.*

The Heroine's Journey is a map to do this. We will need to Leap across Thresholds, not knowing what's on the other side. There will be fear and trembling. But every Leap will bring us closer to discovering what we need to make it through the Belly of the Whale, in order to be reborn and cast into some new role as women thriving in today's world, whatever that may look like.

Yes, we will meet Dragons, but every Dragon we meet and get to know will help us grow in understanding and strength. Then, onward we'll journey, patting our newly befriended Dragons as we go and crossing the Return Threshold, where we'll collect our hard-earned gifts and then share them with the rest of the world.

Yes, we can heal our collective woundedness or stuck places. This is our job as Heroines: to grow to our full potential. This is what ultimately will save the world. As Joseph Campbell told Bill Moyers, "a vital person vitalizes." Every Heroine brings her own hard-earned vitality into the world.

It's nearing the time when you'll leave this book to go back to your own life of living the Heroine's Journey. But there's a danger in going back to your everyday life: the danger that you'll forget you're a Heroine.

You'll forget you've been on this most amazing Journey—more than once. You'll become buried in Ordinary Life and lose the perspective of the larger story happening to you and to all women. Worse yet, you'll fall into a bemoaning and commiserating trap and focus on what you *don't* want instead of on what you *do* want. You'll forget to Do a Circle!

Work to remember.

Continue with Task Two and write your own Heroine Journey's account to help you to remember. The Hero and Heroine stories contain real-life truths. The answers are within you. You don't need a white steed, a sword or a lance—or silver hands. You need quiet time in your life to hear and access what you already know. Don't look without. Look within.

Once it's clear what you're being called to do, take heart! Know that you're supported by all the Heroines who have done the same and Leap over that Threshold. It's what Heroines do.

We are the Heroine with a Thousand Faces. Our individual faces are different and we each have our own unique value, but we are walking the same road and sharing the same Journey. Heroines are needed now more than ever. Share your Journey stories with other Heroines. Let's create a groundswell of women remembering who they really are.

Always remember, you are walking the Road of Adventure, and you are—most assuredly—a Heroine.

The breeze at dawn has secrets to tell you.
Don't go back to sleep.
You must ask for what you really want.
Don't go back to sleep.
People are going back and forth across the
doorsill where the two worlds touch.
The door is round and open.
Don't go back to sleep.

— Rumi, excerpted from "A Great Wagon"

Afterword: My Story

How I Stumbled onto the Yellow Brick Road

As you go the way of life,
You will see a great chasm.
Jump.
It is not as wide as you think.

— Joseph Campbell, *Reflections on the Art of Living*

In January 2007, I left a frigid, winter-bound Maine and flew to sunny, warm Santa Barbara, California, to attend a three-day workshop called *Life Launch: Inspiring New Chapters... A Passionate Guide to the Rest of Your Life.* This workshop, at the Hudson Institute of Santa Barbara, was a prerequisite for enrolling in their year-long executive coaching program, to which I was seriously considering applying. (Executive coaches work one-on-one with a leader of an organization to help him or her move through challenges or improve performance.)

It was during one of the many exercises at this workshop that things began to shift for me. The exercise was called "Life Line." We were asked to draw a line on a large piece of paper and chart our life's big "ups" (to go above the line) and big "downs" (to go below the line). I did the exercise, thinking how I had done similar things before in various other workshops. On my paper, I noted the birth of my children, my divorce, my second marriage and my mother's passing only eight months earlier. I made an entry for leaving the large manufacturing company where I had worked for twelve years (the one I left with Brenda). I had a lot to record. In our small group, we each had a turn to put our paper up on the wall and comment on it. When it was my turn I got up, taped my paper to the wall, explained to the group my life's ups and downs, and then returned to my seat.

It was then that I saw what I had neglected to note on my chart: my current employment—the consulting firm that had been integral to my life for the last eight years—wasn't on my life line!

What? How could that even be?

I had noted all the other big and little employments I had had over the years: teaching jobs, waiting tables during my college summers, and my long stint at the manufacturing company. But my current job wasn't there!

Interesting.

On the third day of the workshop, we were asked to write ourselves a postcard from the future, to write out a picture of our life from the viewpoint of the person we wanted to become. Our future could be defined as anywhere from three months to three years from that day. It was a personal choice. I chose to go out two years and write from the perspective of January 2009. I began writing, and soon my future self was informing me that I would leave my consulting firm in March 2008... a little over a year from when I was writing.

No, wait a minute. That can't be...

But we were supposed to let our writing flow and not critique it. That's what came up, so I wrote it down, even though it clearly wasn't how I pictured my life going.

The workshop was great. It successfully motivated me to matriculate into the Hudson coaching program. I'd be coming back to Santa Barbara for four more weeks throughout the year and graduating in December. I told myself that I was doing this to add executive coaching to my résumé at the consulting firm. (Yes, the one I had forgotten to put on my chart.) I'd then be able to continue to offer my organizational consulting services as well as be a coach. I'd be more marketable. Yes, it was a good business decision.

At some point during that plane ride home to Maine, the wheels in my mind and heart started turning. I had a subtle feeling that I had outgrown my current job. Somewhere between California and Maine, an idea dropped in, the idea that I could (and should) leave my consulting firm *that year* in March 2007! Yes, that very year. (An A+ to those of you who recognize this as a Call.)

Hold on! This would be a big, big Leap!

The Leap was daunting. I had no other job lined up. I'd have to find clients again. I'd have no biweekly paycheck or person to do my billing. There would be no well-known firm to lend me its marketing and name recognition. This would be a Leap into the void.

It would be a solitary Leap.

Studying for a year with the Hudson Institute and acquiring my coaching certification would be like going for my master's degree, I reasoned. Over the years, I had taken plenty of courses to supplement my organizational consulting practice, especially in the mediation and conflict field. But life hadn't opened up a space for a graduate degree. This could be it. I figured my clients would remain with the consulting firm. I had even trained the perfect person to take my place. I could continue organizational development consulting on my own, while focusing on coaching and on my side business, Ruby Slippers, LLC, which provided self-development workshops for women.

I did it! I left the consulting firm in April 2007 to venture out on my own. I was still consulting, but now as a sole practitioner.

I wasn't even halfway through my coaching certification program when I crossed that imaginary Threshold. I felt... excited, like I was unloading an old coat that didn't suit me anymore. It wasn't so scary. I had the framework of the coaching studies in which to operate, so it didn't feel like free fall. And somehow, work kept coming to me. My old clients stayed with the firm, and some new consulting gigs appeared. Money kept coming in. My Leap was working.

Meanwhile, one of the many assignments for the coaching program was to write a final paper and present it to the class by the end of the year. We had to choose our topic and vet it with our school-assigned coach by midyear. It was August and so far, I had no topic.

Of course, it had to be about coaching, and the particular perspective we would bring to the field. Some of my ambitious, organized classmates had already written their papers and presented them in our July session. Always the procrastinator, I couldn't seem to get motivated to start the paper. To make matters worse, I couldn't even figure out what I wanted to write about.

Out of the blue—how many times do we use that phrase when serendipitous forces are at play?—a friend called to tell me that the next day a woman was going to speak about *The Wizard of Oz* in a town up the coast from me.

"Susanna," my friend said, "this speaker shows how the story *The Wizard of Oz* fits into the pattern of the Hero's Journey as Joseph Campbell wrote about it. She's good. I know how much you like *The Wizard of Oz*. You should come."

I didn't want to. The weather was unbearably hot and the presentation was an hour away. But the idea stayed with me. It wouldn't go away even after I tried to reason it away, what with the heat, the distance... oh, yeah, and the awful tourist traffic! True, I loved *The Wizard of Oz*. (After all, I had named my women's workshop and retreat company "Ruby Slippers.") But

I had worked all day and I knew next to nothing about Joseph Campbell. Couldn't I just sit at home?

Apparently, I couldn't. I drove up the coast—heat, traffic and all. Listening to the speaker, Sally Landsburg, talk about Joseph Campbell and the Hero's Journey was life-changing for me. This was the first time I had seen the Hero's Journey laid out and relayed in detail.

Sally explained the milestones of Dorothy's Journey:

- The tornado? It brings Dorothy into Oz. She's Crossing the Threshold and entering on her Journey into the unknown.

- Toto? That's Dorothy's intuition. He guides her, always leading her to the next step.

Sally's use of *The Wizard of Oz* as her example of a Hero's Journey couldn't have been more meaningful to me, especially since it was the story that I used with my workshop attendees to talk about our own lives. I learned that the Hero(ine)'s Journey is the underlying theme in the books and movies that I like the most: those in which the main characters transform. And Campbell laid out the path of transformation! It connected the dots for me... my love of literature, transformation and the yellow brick road of growth that we all have within us. I felt a little awestruck as I watched different parts of my life connecting together!

It was an a-ha moment for me. And here I was, studying to be a coach to help others have those same a-ha moments that would transform their lives! "Serendipitous" doesn't even begin to describe it.

I also knew I had found the topic for my final paper: how can we, as coaches, help clients see their Hero(ine)'s Journey? For me, the model of the Heroine's Journey had become the basic tool in the transformative process of coaching. I was inspired!

And then came yet another moment of great serendipity. I was required, as part of the coaching certification program, to find a

Hudson Institute coach who would coach *me* for the rest of the program. I approached the Hudson president, sharing with her my newfound passion for the Heroine's Journey and my decision to make it the topic for my final paper.

She immediately recommended Dr. Pat Adson, a psychologist and author who was equally passionate about the Hero's Journey, to be my coach. Then and there, I was matched with the perfect person to guide me down this new path that was unfolding under my feet in a very yellow brick road–like way.

At the end of the program, the reviewers at Hudson gave me high marks for my paper and accompanying presentation, which, of course, I called "Finding My Own Ruby Slippers." Looking back with the wisdom of hindsight, I recognize that that paper planted the seed for this book.

With the program behind me, I put all that I had learned into action as I continued to grow my consulting and executive coaching business (Liller Consulting, LLC) and my women's workshops and retreats business (Ruby Slippers, LLC). I saw clearly that my life and the lives of all those people around me were also examples of individuals living the Heroine's (and Hero's) Journey. We were all living this inspiring and transformational pattern!

In my coaching, I knew that I could talk about life challenges and never mention the Heroine's Journey, but I came to realize that there is power in knowing, and seeing oneself in, the Heroine archetype. Why did those ancient storytellers continue to tell this tale of an ordinary person who leaves the village to go on an adventure and who returns with something that benefits all, if it wasn't to illustrate important life principles?

I wanted women to recognize this and see the Heroine's Journey as:

- a meaningful *guide* to use as they follow their intuition and try what they haven't before (even if it's small).

- a *lens* to view life's challenges as necessary because those challenges develop the individual. It's about finding the lessons and seeing the gifts in every situation.

- an *invitation* to eventually discover or uncover their unique gifts, reaping the rewards if they take the Journey.

The Heroine archetype so deeply resonated with me that, frankly, I just had to share it with other women. I couldn't stop talking about it. There had been so many times in my own life that I had left the comfort of the known and leaped into the unknown. I was still doing it! I saw how the risks I had taken had made me a much more confident woman. I wanted other women to experience that same awareness. I was determined that every woman would know about the Heroine's Journey! And that, my friends, was the Journey that led to *writing this book.*

Thank you for reading *You Are a Heroine.* If you've enjoyed this book please leave a review on your favorite book-related site. It helps me reach more people so they too can begin their own Heroine's Journey.

Meet the Real-Life Heroines

Pamela McCreary is the award-winning author of the memoir *Dancing on the Head of a Pin*. She has been a professional actor in Denver for the last thirty-plus years, appearing in numerous television commercials, a few television shows, a video on MTV (no lace or leather was involved), corporate films and voice-  overs, as well as the Disney Channel original movie *Lemonade Mouth*.

Her greatest passion is empowering others, especially women. She volunteers with several organizations and speaks to women's groups, offering strategies for creating joy and strength in the now. Pamela serves on the board of The Initiative, an organization whose mission is creating an abuse-free culture for all (dviforwomen.org). For more information, visit pamelamccreary.com.

Maureen Manley is a well-respected speaker, life coach, educator and consultant. Her company, Spirit In Motion, offers a variety of thought-provoking and engaging experiences that explore a multidisciplinary approach to fostering greater personal power and creative potential. Maureen provides realistic and

practical understandings to assist in moving you forward as a whole person, with an empowered approach to clarifying and then creating what you desire. Learn more about her at maureenmanley.com.

 As a healing artist, adventurer and life coach, **Lisa Chu** creates experiences that support and encourage people of all ages to rediscover creativity, reclaim spirit, and live with greater joy, peace and freedom. Her offerings include workshops, speaking and one-on-one coaching. Learn more about her life-coaching practice at themusicwithinus.com.

She is also a practicing visual artist and illustrator, celebrating the unexpected through her creative process at wildtomatoarts.com. Follow her daily art-making on Instagram/Twitter (@drlisachu).

For her ongoing musical appearances as an acoustic rock violinist, visit chinesemelodrama.com.

Acknowledgments

(This list is lengthy because, in true Heroine's Journey style, there are so many people who have helped me along the way!)

Katy Harkleroad, the best-ever editor, is a mentor if there ever was one. I never saw her magic wand, but its effect is evident throughout this book. I couldn't have written and finished it without her. Thank you for believing in me and in my book, Katy.

Jack Barnard started it all. Jack is the book coach who got me to start writing (after giving me some much-needed kicks in the rear to get there). He saw some little seeds in me and helped me plant and cultivate them. Now, those seeds have blossomed into this book (and so much other writing). This book couldn't have happened without you either, Jack. Thank you for your honesty and willingness to always call me on my stuff!

Patty Lennon, I thank divine providence for ending up next to you in that circle at the Chi Center so I could hear you say, "Give your book over to an expert." You told me then you had the perfect people in mind. That wisdom felt so right and as soon as I got back to Maine I contacted Tara R. Alemany and Mark Gerber of Emerald Lake Books. Their expertise and experience, especially with the business end of selling books, was exactly what my book and I needed. Patty, Tara and Mark, you all have been a godsend.

Thank you to my family and friends who kept asking, "How's the book going?" You have continued to root for me as the years(!) went by. You are the loving support that has sustained me on every Journey. Creighton Taylor and Amy Wood, we really did help women attract the lives they wanted. You two helped me see what was possible. I owe you both so much.

Special thanks to Tina Campidelli, my agent in the world as I offered courses and retreats for Heroines. Much gratitude to you, Barbara Babkirk, for your mentorship and for inviting me to facilitate with you on your women's retreats in France! Also, to Brady Nickerson, for coming with me on the retreat and work-shop circuit to teach Heroines how to unfold themselves through your beautiful intuitive painting process. Priscilla Grant has been there for me and the book since the beginning. Thank you, Priscilla, for your artful and kind editing and suggestions. Elizabeth Margolis-Pineo, another person who has been with me since the beginning, designing every workbook, flyer, business card and more through every new iteration of Ruby Slippers. Thank you, Libby, for your guiding creative and always-fun presence as we journeyed together.

Thank you to my son, Stephen Card, who lovingly pushed and tugged at me to get my Heroine's Journey courses out into the world and especially online. I hope you know how much you did for me. And much gratitude to Courtney Card, who laboriously transcribed all those Heroine stories without me even asking! Your partnership in this with me is one of the high points in my life. My daughter, Laurel Card, lives the Heroine's life daily, setting the example for her daughter and for everyone she meets. I thought of you often as I wrote this book, Laurel. All the conversations we had about the Journey aided me greatly in my writing. Thank you. And please don't tell anyone that you have clearly identified me as a Threshold Guardian. Yikes! Let's just remember how Heroines are continually learning, and I still am!

Pamela, Maureen and Lisa, thank you for your trust in me and your willingness to be in my book in all your wise and vulnerable glory. Your stories were such an inspiration to me and to those who heard them on the broadcast. They just had to be in the book. And I extend much gratitude to Gail Larsen, teacher extraordinaire, creator of the Transformational Speaking Immersion course where I met Maureen and Lisa.

I am grateful to all the Heroines who came to my workshops and retreats. You know who you are. Thank you also to the many Heroines I interviewed who don't appear in this book but whose willingness to share their stories with me contributed greatly to my understanding of how women take the Journey. The material in this book is the result of the sharing and learning that happens whenever and wherever Heroines gather together. I am most grateful that we found a meeting place for a while—a crossroads on our respective journeys.

Robin Liller, the Journey with you has been nothing short of amazing. You are my pragmatist, my rational thinker, and my biggest link to common sense. If it weren't for you, I'd be lost in la-la land, for sure. You balance me in all the right places. You're my hero.

About the Author

Susanna Liller, like many women, wears multiple professional hats (which she enjoys wearing). She is an organizational-development consultant, executive coach, women's workshop leader, writer and musician. Her career, whether mediating, facilitating or coaching with groups or individuals, has  always been about helping people find the path that evolves them to the next level of success. She believes that everyone's journey in work and life exists to transform them to a higher level of being. The challenge, however, is to not resist the change. Susanna sees herself as a guide and motivator in this transformational process.

Susanna lives on a small farm in Maine along with her husband Robin, four overfed sheep, a one-eyed rooster, two chatty hens, Merlin the cross-eyed Maine Coon cat, and a wimpy one-hundred-dred-pound dog named Max. She spends as much time as she can visiting her children and grandchildren. In her "spare" time, Susanna plays the keyboard and sings in a band, which has landed her in the Belly of the Whale more than once! She loves seeing every day as an adventure on her own life Journey.

If you're interested in having Susanna come speak to your group or organization, you can contact her at emeraldlakebooks.com/liller.

Suggested Reading
for Your Heroine's Journey

Adson, Patricia R. 1999. *A Princess and Her Garden: A Fable of Awakening and Arrival*. Red Wing, Minnesota: Lone Oak Press, Ltd.

———. 2004. *Depth Coaching: Discovering Archetypes for Empowerment, Growth and Balance*. Gainesville, Florida: Center for Applications of Psychological Type, Inc.

Bolen, Jean Shinoda. 2004. *Crossing to Avalon: A Woman's Midlife Quest for the Sacred Feminine*. San Francisco, California: HarperOne.

Campbell, Joseph. 1991. *Reflections on the Art of Living, A Joseph Campbell Companion*. New York Harper Perennial.

———. 2008. *The Hero with a Thousand Faces*. Novato, California: New World Library.

Campbell, Joseph, and Bill Moyers. 1988. *The Power of Myth*. New York: Doubleday.

Estés, Clarissa Pinkola. 1996. *Women Who Run with the Wolves: Myths and Stories of the Wild Woman Archetype*. New York City: Ballantine Books.

Frankel, Valerie Estelle. 2010. *From Girl to Goddess: The Heroine's Journey through Myth and Legend*. Jefferson, North Carolina: McFarland & Company, Inc.

Harris, Reg, and Susan Thompson. 1995. *The Hero's Journey: A Guide to Literature and Life.* Napa, California: Harris Communications.

Jeffers, Susan. 2003. *Embracing Uncertainty: Breakthrough Methods for Achieving Peace of Mind When Facing the Unknown.* New York: St. Martin's Press.

Murdock, Maureen. 1990. *The Heroine's Journey: Woman's Quest for Wholeness.* Boston: Shambhala Publications.

Myss, Caroline. 2007. *Entering the Castle: An Inner Path to God and Your Soul.* New York: Simon & Schuster.

Pearson, Carol S. 1998. *The Hero Within: Six Archetypes We Live By.* New York: HarperCollins.

Endnotes

1. Joseph Campbell, *Pathway to Bliss: Mythology and Personal Transformation* (Novato, CA: New World Library, 2004), 113.

2. John P. Schuster, *Answering Your Call: A Guide for Living Your Deepest Purpose,* 1st ed. (San Francisco: Berrett-Koehler Publishers, 2003), 5–6.

3. Peter S. Beagle, *The Last Unicorn,* 40th Anniversary ed. (London: Penguin Books, 2008), 251.

4. Joseph Campbell, *The Hero with a Thousand Faces* (Novato, CA: New World Library, 2008), 42.

5. Friedemann Wieland, *The Journey of the Hero: Personal Growth, Deep Ecology and the Quest for the Grail* (New York: Prism Press, 1994), 7.

6. Schuster, *Answering Your Call,* 20.

7. *The Croods,* directed by Kirk DeMicco and Chris Sanders (March 22, 2013; Glendale, CA: DreamWorks Animation, October 1, 2013), DVD.

8. Susanna Liller, *Circle Power: Connecting to Something Greater* (Bath, ME: Susanna Liller, 2010).

9. Jack Kent, *There's No Such Thing as a Dragon* (New York: Random House Children's Books, 2005).

THE WORLD NEEDS HEROINES!

Encourage yourself and others to heed The Call!

Available for purchase now!
susannaliller.com/tshirt

Please visit us at
emeraldlakebooks.com

EMERALD LAKE
BOOKS

CPSIA information can be obtained
at www.ICGtesting.com
Printed in the USA
LVHW010925290620
659221LV00009B/1037

9 781945 847073